P. 164

P g - Magic Circle

How to Use ESP

How to Use
ESP

The Hidden Power of Your Mind

Dorothy Spence Lauer
with Brad Steiger

2002
Galde Press, Inc.
PO Box 460, Lakeville, Minnesota 55044–0460, U.S.A.

First Galde Press Edition
Third Printing, 2002

This book has been updated from the original edition of 1969
published by Lancer Books, Inc., New York.

Library of Congress Cataloging-in-Publication Data
  Lauer, Dorothy Spence.
      How to use ESP : the hidden power of your mind / Dorothy
  Spence Lauer : with Brad Steiger. — 1st Galde Press ed.
          p.   cm.
      ISBN 1–880090–51–1 (pbk.)
      1. Extrasensory perception.   2. Psychic ability.   I. Steiger,
  Brad.   II. Title.
  BF1321.L33   1998
  133.8—dc21   98–10396
                                                              CIP

Galde Press, Inc.
PO Box 460
Lakeville, Minnesota 55044

Tributes to the Phenomenal Dorothy Spence Lauer—One of the Great Psychics of Our Time

"Those wonderful readings of yours!"

"You are remarkable!"

"I am amazed at the accuracy of the aura analysis you did for me!"

Excerpts from hundreds of grateful letters testify to Dorothy Spence Lauer's astonishing ability not only to predict events in people's lives, but to recognize, evaluate, and encourage their own hidden talents for extrasensory perception—in many cases, on the basis of correspondence only…

Here, with the story of her amazing career by famed parapsychologist Brad Steiger, Mrs. Lauer shows how you, too, can get what you want out of life through ESP. Her book is more than a thrilling reading experience. It is a step-by-step guide to happiness you may only have dreamed of—a guide to riches you will never forget.

Contents

Introduction

The Amazing World of Dorothy Spence Lauer

J n the March 1964 issue of *Search* magazine, editor Ray Palmer presented a tribute to the incredible ability of Dorothy Spence Lauer to predict the future.

"Thus, we knew that Dorothy was predicting the death of the President [John F. Kennedy]. In fact, she had warned us several times during the past three years that [he] would die. She was right about the Pope. She was right about several movie stars. She has been right about several of our readers, whom she mentioned sadly to us, saying she simply couldn't tell them what she was in their aura, or in their handwriting…

> *We have been publishing the predictions of Dorothy Lauer for nearly ten years now. During that time she has established herself as the most accurate prognosticator we have ever encountered.* [This is high praise coming from an editor whose magazine has published accounts of nearly every major seer of both historical and contemporary times.]

We have many hundreds of letters in our files from people she has helped. Not only does she predict, but she advises. Her advice is something that it is well to follow. She has [the client] at heart.

Those who have received psychometry readings from her know the time and effort she spends on each reading. One thing is certain, Dorothy Lauer will never get rich at her task; because unlike a great number of so-called prophets...every letter is personal and typed by either herself or a secretary, in the latter case, from diction. The time she spends on these letters is tremendous, and we often wonder how she has the stamina to continue it.

It seems traditional for any self-respecting psychic to claim that he was born with a "mystic cross" on his palm or that she was the seventh daughter of a seventh daughter. Dorothy Spence Lauer made no claims that any stars fell on the night of her birth. She was grateful that she managed to survive the birth experience at all.

Dorothy's mother was unaware of the fact that she was pregnant until she fainted at the end of a roller coaster ride in an amusement park. Although Mr. Spence was startled by his wife's reaction to the ride, she shrugged and said, "Let's go on it again; maybe I was just frightened."

When she fainted dead away a second time, Mr. Spence insisted that she see a doctor.

"Mrs. Spence," the doctor smiled at her upon his completion of her examination, "do you know that you are going to have a baby in three months' time?"

Mrs. Spence left the office complaining to her husband that their family doctor had better brush up on his knowledge of pregnancy. She, about to have a baby? Preposterous. "It's so incredible, so ridiculous that I simply won't believe it!" she told Mr. Spence.

Three months later to the day, April 2, 1909, Mrs. Spence gave birth to a baby daughter, whom they named Dorothy.

No, Dorothy was not born with any mystic symbols printed upon her infant body. For one thing, there would hardly have been room for even one decent pentagram. Dorothy weighed only a pound and half and measured just eleven inches.

"My mother often told me how my father would actually put me in his coat pocket," Dorothy recalled. "Whenever Mother would enter a store with me, the managers would often ask us to leave because of the commotion that would be raised when people would gather around to see such a tiny baby."

Even today with the modern incubation facilities available in our hospitals, a baby of such diminutive size does not always survive. Because she did survive against such a handicap, Dorothy has long felt that she was given a mission in life.

"When I was only five or six, I began to realize that I had certain feelings that no one else had. I would freely state the impressions which I received by handling various personal objects of my parents' friends. There were many times that my mother left me at home because she was afraid that perhaps I might tell people things that would embarrass them. As I grew older, I realized the wisdom of her decision."

Throughout her school days, Dorothy was always "feeling" things about her classmates and teachers. "But my mother warned me never to make myself obvious in any way, nor to behave in such a manner as to bring ridicule upon the wonderful gift that I had been given. I learned to say little or nothing about my impressions to my classmates, but when I returned home after school, I would sit and pour out my feelings to my mother.

"I have always thanked my mother for making me realize that a person with a true psychic gift need not in any way appear odd or strange or behave in any manner different from anyone else."

Dorothy's school days were happy ones, and she found an outlet for her psychism in music. She attended grammar school, high school, and one year of college; then for a period of time, she taught music.

"But in school and later when I taught, my mind was most often on those feelings that I had within me. I read a great deal, but it was my music that helped me over the feeling of not being able to express myself as I truly desired. I was forced to repress my psychic gift, but my music allowed me to express my moods in a socially acceptable manner at practically any time I wished."

Dorothy continued to repress her psychic talents with only occasional readings for a select circle of clients. Then, as she recalls, "This wonderful friend that I had in Chicago, who has guided me in many respects, told me that I would not be able to lay this work aside. The day would come that I would have to give my complete attention to it.

"During the time my children were small, I did not give readings on a large scale. I kept my clientele very limited. But once my children were grown, I became totally committed to helping others with ESP."

As Ray Palmer, editor of *Search* magazine, noted in the article from which I quoted at the beginning of this introduction, Dorothy Lauer gave generously of her time and her psychic energies to her clientele, whom she regarded as beloved friends. At my continued urging, Dorothy reluctantly allowed me to read some of the thousands of letters which she receives from individuals whom she has been allowed to aid through the medium of her psychic gift.

A Miss S.C. from Columbia, South Carolina, writes:

> I would like to take this opportunity to thank you for the great service and advice which you have given to so many people. Your God-given gift has done wonders…for so many troubled souls. I can say this from my own experience. This last aura analysis has been so accurate.
>
> I once had a teacher who always said, "Give credit where credit is due." Although I realize that each individual must and *does* bring on the happenings in his life, credit must, however, be given to the person who helps in influencing that life. That person is you, Mrs. Lauer. I also know that you would never accept any personal praise. You, too, would "give credit where credit is due." Thank you again. You are truly a great humanitarian.

Mrs. C.H. from St. Paul, Minnesota, wrote to inform Dorothy that a series of predictions which she had made years before had now nearly all come to pass.

Mr. H.T.L. of West Virginia told Dorothy that her long-range analysis had been realized with one hundred percent accuracy:

> I divided your [analysis] into twenty predictions. *All* of these are understandable now. Three were in the nature of warnings. Two of these appeared quickly, but worked out all right—probably because I followed your advice. The third has not yet taken place, probably because I was forewarned by you and took definite steps to prevent it!
>
> Of the seventeen remaining predictions, *all* have applied! Some were of great importance, some of lesser, but they have all been working out—some quickly, some over a period of years. Two were given in a symbolism that I understood perfectly.
>
> The quickest one was the one about back pain. I had already suffered this—nothing permanent, but quite painful at the time. I did have it taken care of by a "competent physician," who ordered me to do no work the day following his treatment. I spent the greater part of that day writing my first letter to you, so your reply contained an immediate on-target item that I did not have to wait for!
>
> I hope that the above method of classifying your letter into categories doesn't seem too mechanical. It is my way of explaining what a *good* analysis you gave me and pointing out that I consider your comments to constitute a series of 100% "hits." Certainly nobody could argue that *percentage* could be due to lucky chance!

A Dr. M.B.W. of Oxford, Michigan, took time from his practice to write a letter verifying the accuracy of the predictions which Dorothy had made for him.

When I was on the Board of Directors of_____, I told you that, in my opinion, the executive secretary was working for himself and not for the betterment of the association. As you predicted, he was dismissed at our fall meeting.

You spoke in your last letter of my seeing a dentist. Well, it wasn't a week from that date that I had an abscessed tooth develop and it had to be pulled.

In the same letter you also stated that I might have to appear in court as an expert witness. Here again on the same day that your letter arrived, I got two phone calls on two different cases to testify in court.

Señor P.C. of Caracas, Venezuela, wrote Dorothy to confirm her grim prediction of an earthquake in his country.

This is a little word to tell you that we all came out sound and safe from the terrible earthquakes which shook Caracas on last Saturday night. We were at home and it was quite frightening to see this building jerking as it did.

Strangely enough, I had just reread the letter you wrote warning me of a possible earthquake. During the quake, I remembered your letter and I felt quieter.

The building where we live was not at all damaged. Probably a few hundred among two or three thousand buildings in Caracas are damaged, but nothing too grave, and they will be repaired as soon as possible. Unfortunately, a few buildings at the seashore fell apart instantly, killing many people. The total casualties amount to over 250 victims.

I suppose you did not worry too much about us, as I tried to send you some thoughts by telepathy.

Occasionally, Dorothy is asked to give an analysis for a woman who is eager to know what Cupid has in store for her. As usual, Dorothy's advice is astonishingly accurate.

Mrs. D.W.B. of Riverside, California, wrote:

The man beside me is my husband, the one you told me three years ago would be standing at my side. At that time I did not know he existed. Today we are very happily married. I thought you might like to know that your prediction came true—even though I was certain at the time you gave it that it would never be!

In the August 1961 issue of *Exploring the Unknown,* Vance L. Milligan tells in his article, "The Amazing Dorothy Spence Lauer," of an analysis which Dorothy made for him.

I recall giving the letter to my wife Evelyn and seeing her expression change from nonchalant interest to utter amazement. "How in the world could she know all this about you?"

I answered, "This is an amazing person."

Dorothy had begun Milligan's analysis by telling him that she saw a man who would surprise the writer by offering him an advancement that would greatly increase his earning capacity. She went on to state that even though Milligan would feel he was not capable of the demands of the job, he would be foolish to refuse such an opportunity, as it involved his future security.

"She stated that light pink in my aura revealed these things to her," Milligan says. "She wrote that a deep pink color revealed I would have to change some plan. She stated that she had a deep feeling that this detour of plans would come about as a result of this offer, but the advancement was more important."

Dorothy next analyzed a copper-colored hue in Milligan's aura as being indicative of a man who worked closely with the writer, who would "speak very highly" of him when the advancement would be offered.

According to Milligan:

> The amazing story is, at the time, I had recently resigned my pastorate of St Paul's A.M.E. Church in Circleville, Ohio, so that I could enroll in Wilberforce College.
>
> I took a job at a local rubber factory to provide support for my family and expense money for my college studies…A personal friendship…developed between Deacon Lewis Adams and myself because of our mutual interest in religion.…This relationship led to an invitation to visit his pastor, Dr. U.S. Munnerlyn [who] was in need of an assistant.

Milligan had no idea that he would be considered for the job, because he was an ordained Elder in the Methodist Church and he felt that his qualifications were inadequate. But he writes:

Mrs. Lauer was wrong only on the point that I would be surprised when the man made the offer for advancement. Two days after I received the aura analysis, Mr. Adams came to me and told me that Dr. Munnerlyn was greatly impressed with me, and that he was considering me as an assistant. Consequently, I was not surprised. I knew what to expect when Pastor Munnerlyn called me into his study to make the offer on the Sunday that followed. I inwardly smiled and thought, Dorothy Spence Lauer is an amazing person.

Milligan concurs that Dorothy's predictions were accurate in every other way. He was successful in his new position. The advancement greatly increased his earning capacity. His future security had been enriched. He had to change his plans for entering college, and a man with whom he worked had recommended him for the position.

Just how did Dorothy Spence Lauer work these minor miracles for her clients? How was she able to "tune in" on people whom she may never meet in person and give them personal predictions of amazing accuracy?

Dorothy was a psychometrist who specialized in precognition; that is, foreseeing the future. According to Ray Palmer, who published Dorothy's column and studied her abilities for more than a decade, "Ordinarily she needs but an object belonging to, or handled by, the subject, or the presence of the subject, to become aware of the psychic influences from which she draws her information. However, by writing out a verse, while concentrating, a prospective client can produce a sufficiently powerful psychic impression to enable her to receive the information she seeks."

Palmer has admitted that he began the examination of Dorothy Spence Lauer's talents as a "deliberate project," and "we [*Search* magazine] feel proud to know that we have proved psychometry a reality."

Later in her life, Dorothy was no longer able to grant many personal readings and analyses because of the great press of her work. She did, however, welcome the opportunity to provide analyses by mail, and she gained a clientele of several thousand. Dorothy offered two basic services, a psychometric analysis and a photo aura analysis. For the psychometric analysis, she asked that a client select a short verse from the Bible and write it on a sheet of paper while concentrating on his problems. To obtain a photo aura analysis, the client could simply send a snapshot of himself to Mrs. Lauer.

As might be expected, every so often Dorothy found that she was being "tested" by a skeptic who is eager to debunk her to the "credulous dupes" who consult her. In one such case, I learned of a cynical woman who had a friend write a Bible verse to which she signed her name. The skeptic was certain that such a maneuver would confuse the psychometrist. After all, if one woman wrote the specimen and another signed her name, on whose psychic vibrations would the seer "tune in"? One woman is asking for help, but she is requesting this aid in another's handwriting. It would seem that whatever the psychometrist would answer would be off target, which to the narrow mind of of skeptic would, of course, prove that the psychic had no real ability at all.

Dorothy Spence Lauer did not claim to be infallible, but her psychic abilities must have been glowing red-hot on the day that she received the deceitful letter which had been carefully designed to "test" her. According to a third party—a sincere and devoted client of Mrs. Lauer's who was terribly disturbed that her friend had sought to pull off such a sneaky bit of debunking—Dorothy gave an accurate account of the woman who had held the writing instrument, including her husband's occupation and certain intimate matters, and passed on some advice to the perpetrator of the hoax that was so personal, "it scared her half to death!"

Dorothy never denied that she had her "misses" as well as her "hits," but those who relied on her psychic advice for over forty years regarded her as a truly sincere and accomplished seer and guide. The letter from Mrs. H.B.L. of Ft. Lauderdale, Florida, seems representative of the several hundred testimonials which I read while helping Dorothy prepare this book:

They can have Nostradamus; they can have Mother Shipton; they can even have the much-touted Jeanne Dixon. *I'll* take Dorothy Spence Lauer every time!

Yes, sir, "on a clear day she can see forever." In fact, she can even see loud and clear on a "foggy day in London town" or on a smoggy day in other towns of great renown.

Her misses are few—at least for me—and I am sure there are many satisfied customer who will make the same claim. Her hits are many, and I believe in telling her when she sees true.

How fortunate I am to have a companion like Dorothy Spence Lauer as I travel the Path.

When *How to Use ESP* was published in 1969, Dorothy Spence Lauer soon became a companion on the Path to hundreds of thousands of other men and women who were as delighted as Mrs. H.B.L. to declare her prophetic insights superior to those of other seers. Within a few years, the book had sold an astonishing million copies in paperback.

I had always respected Dorothy's abilities as a psychic-sensitive, and I had been greatly impressed by the down-to-earth simplicity of her teachings and the marvelous effectiveness of her mental techniques, but I must admit that I had not foreseen such an incredible response to Dorothy Spence Lauer's powerful lessons in psychic development. *How to Use ESP* went back to press again and again as her Golden Magic Circle reached out and brought peace, hope, love, and, yes, prosperity to thousands of readers throughout North and South America. It was as if she were offering proven metaphysical formulas that could truly work for every sincere practitioner of her teachings.

Testimonial after tribute poured into my office as well as her own, and it was thrilling to read the hundreds of accounts of those who had achieved access to the hidden power of their minds through Dorothy's guidance. It is, in fact, due to the generosity of one such reader that this present edition has come into being for a new generation of students who may benefit from Dorothy's practical wisdom.

Our benefactor, who wishes to remain anonymous, says that it is her desire to "honor Mrs. Lauer's deep dedication of her life's work for the benefit of humankind."

Continuing, the devoted student writes, "I was one who was blessed by Dorothy Spence Lauer's work, and I now feel privileged to have a tiny part in seeing that her light may continue to shine forth so that others may also find their way to a higher awareness and be blessed."

And now, dear reader, the great adventure lies ahead of you. Allow the proven techniques of this most remarkable lady to guide you on the path to another dimension of reality where you may come face to face with your true essence and potentials—the *you* that was truly meant to be. Permit Dorothy Spence Lauer to show you how to touch the farthest parameters of your being and the Source of All That Is through the hidden power of your mind.

—BRAD STEIGER

October 1997

Preface

This book has come to be written because of the thousands of requests which I have received over the years to actually put my psychic techniques into book form. Each chapter has been carefully developed and the information imparted therein is composed of time-tested working formulas.

As you read this book, I wish that you would sit comfortably in a chair and picture me sitting next to you. It was for you that I wrote this book. It is to you that I direct every comment. Keep this book by your bedside if at all possible. First read it thoroughly, then proceed each night to glimpse through it as you desire. This is very important, because such a procedure will permit your subconscious to take over and to record many of the vital matters that I do want you to keep in mind.

In this book, I want very much to convey a clearer understanding of the occult, or psychomagnetism, than most people have now. The world of extrasensory perception, ESP, need not be a mysterious and veiled subject. Once you have read this book, I know that you will have gained all the information needed to practice each psychic talent and to master it. The various mystery schools, the several secret societies, and the many alleged psychic development courses would not only bring you great expense, but in the end you would discover that every bit of mystic knowledge bequeathed to you had already been covered and outlined in this book.

By reading and practicing the techniques offered in this book, you may be sure that you can bring practically anything into your life that you desire. So very few people understand or realize that in many instances they have the power to control their own destiny. The prospect of controlling one's fate will present a challenge which I know that you will meet with courage. By the time you finish reading this book, there should be no doubt left in your mind that you will be able to get what you want out of life through ESP.

The chapters in this book have been arranged in such a manner that you will be able to understand all the techniques perfectly. If so many of my clients were not already reaping the benefits from these techniques, this book would never have been written. You may rest assured that this book will begin to open a new doorway for you with the reading of the very first chapter. You will soon discover that the key to success in life lies within you.

—DOROTHY SPENCE LAUER

Chapter One

Achieving Success With the Golden Magic Circle

There is a ritual described in this chapter that should enable you to successfully utilize the Golden Magic Circle. In addition to the ritual, there are a number of psychic exercises. I suggest that as you follow through with these experiments, you keep a record of your accomplishments. I am asking the publisher to place an extra page at the end of this chapter with nothing but the word "Notes" printed on it. On this page you may jot down exactly what things came to you as a result of using this ritual and these exercises, and may I suggest that you record the date for each application of these psychic formulas.

The Golden Magic Circle has brought many wonderful things to many people's lives, and it can do the same for you. You may find that at first you will feel your gains and successes will be too good to be true. Remember, everything that I have included in this book has first been worked out through my own experience and is a compilation of my own success formulas.

The Golden Magic Circle has no beginning and no end. Therefore, remember that to use such a force in the wrong manner would bring about a boomerang effect. If you should profane this force in any way, that which you misuse, whether it is a thought, a word, or an action toward any person, will, instead of acting upon that person, return upon you. I write this caution because, I am sorry to say, there are some people who are unscrupulous, and that is why I place this warning at the beginning of this chapter.

I wish to make it perfectly clear that I am not a superstitious person, but there are certain laws of the universe which can bring about their own price of retribution if they should be violated. The age-old saying "Whatsoever a man soweth, that shall he also reap—very much applies here. Neither am I exempt from these cosmic laws of retribution because I am engaged in psychic work. That is why I am so very, very cautious in my thoughts.

This does not mean that I cannot become angry or have the thoughts that all mortal men have. But it does mean that since I know the power of this cosmic law, I am more liable to be just a little more careful than would be people who may not be as aware of such a force. By the same token, always keep in mind that the good thoughts which you send to others are bound to come back to you and bring you only happiness and contentment.

Many times I have had people ask me why I do not use the Golden Magic Circle in gambling, horse racing, and all the games of chance. The Golden Magic Circle is not to be used in this manner.

"Why aren't you a millionaire?" I am constantly being asked by certain types of people. I have no desire to amass great wealth, but if destiny ever should dictate that I was to reach a certain status, I am certain that it would not be through a utilization of my talents for gambling. Such financial reward would be achieved because I put sincere effort into the work that I love so well, and because I used the cosmic laws correctly and constructively.

I do not, of course, condemn others if they should solicit my gifts in an attempt to locate oil or mineral deposits. Here are sections from a letter that such a client, Mr. S.R. of Phoenix, Arizona, wrote me to relay news of his (or should I say "our") success:

> In regard to your analysis report of Sept. 6, 1961…your report was extremely accurate, and more important, the fact that you mentioned the use of a machine or divining rod which would isolate the gold deposit proves your ability. I located this claim with a pendulum, employing the science of radiesthesia.
>
> I have progressed considerably on the claim…building a road…clearing overburden over the vein areas…
>
> I have two professional confirmations from two parties who have agreed on the positions of the veins, the depths, and one has measured the size and has given the value of the major vein, as well as two others. The major vein was valued at $300 a ton, twenty feet down from the present surface…The other veins have a $125 and a $92 a ton value of lesser volume. The base figure or value of all veins is approximately $79,000. It could go well over $100,000.

Mr. S.R. will never doubt that the Golden Magic Circle worked for him. I have never yet seen a person use the Golden Magic Circle without achieving some result. There simply has to be some success! Whatever I tell you in this book has been tested over a period many years, not only by myself but by several thousand of my clients.

I know your first questions to me would be, "Just what is this Golden Magic Circle and what will it do for me?" My answer to that is, this Golden Magic Circle will do much for you. However, you must apply all the instructions diligently and do not consider that the ritual may be accomplished by a mere reading of text.

If you were to come to my home, I would first have you sit very comfortably in a chair and relax completely. In its very simplest form, the Magic Circle is really a concentration of the power of your mind, body, and soul in a radiant, dynamic circle about your body. You will soon discover that it is the force in back of your life; it is the invisible, magnetic power that flows in the universe, which many may channel with his mind and release in a dynamic stream of radiant energy. Yet it is more, ever so much more! It is actually a potent power of God's infinite intelligence as it animates all creation.

The Golden Magic Circle will make you a much different person. Every atom and cell of your brain will become charged with positive thoughts. It will be as if you were going on an adventure when you put this Golden Magic Circle around you. I warn you, though, that after it is once done, do not be surprised if things come to you in the most unexpected ways. You will find opportunities opening to you that have never been put before you heretofore. You will meet many new people, who will seem to come into your life most unexpectedly, yet each and every one of them will be there for a purpose.

I do not think we meet anyone by chance. I think a person is put into our life for a reason. Although it is of no great importance, the following illustration shows how this process works.

Here in California, we never know just when it is going to rain. Even though I had a premonition of rain before I started downtown one afternoon, I pushed it aside, as we all often do, thinking that perhaps my intuition could be wrong. I should know better by now!

Within half an hour, we had a cloudburst. All I had with me were rain boots, which one carries quite frequently during the normal rainy season here. I was thinking that now I would have to stop in the nearest store and get proper rain clothes. Strange as this may sound, I was walking up to the counter to purchase these articles when a woman walked up to me (I could see that she too was headed for the same counter). She said, very nicely, "I wonder if you would mind taking this rain cape I have? I must buy a new one, and it looks as if you were unexpectedly caught in this rain. Would you please take it? I would consider it a favor, indeed. That way, I don't think you would have to go to the expense of another one."

I was taken aback, I must say, and I said to her. "I do have two at home, but I would have bought another because the rain is so very bad."

There, among hundreds of people, the kind woman had circled me out as the one to receive her rain cape.

So you see, the invisible law of supply, even in its simplest form, will work. Had my needs been greater than for a rain cape, those wants too would have been supplied.

I have countless request on file from people who have asked me to place the Golden Magic Circle around them. Sometimes they seem to think that if I place it around them, it will be more powerful than if they do it, but that is not true in any sense.

You will notice that the Golden Magic Circle can also be shared with other people. For instance, whenever I hear an ambulance siren, I send a Golden Magic Circle to that person, hoping it will help them through whatever is ahead of them. I don't have to know the person because I have done this many thousands of times. Once it so happened that one of the people was someone I did know and, as they were being placed in the ambulance, they said they felt a peace of mind come over them that they had never before experienced.

Now, please do not misunderstand me. I do not claim to have any supernatural powers. It is my implicit faith in God that accomplishes these things.

There are those afflicted with cancer who are worried and say that they know someone put a curse on them. The first thing I tell this person is that he must first of all, with his heart, say, "I now place (name or person) lovingly in the hands of the Father. That which is for his own highest good shall come to him." Then, of course, one cannot turn around and add a lot of things that he would like to have happen to the person. If someone has hurt you, cursed you, or caused you any unhappiness in life, you must leave it directly in the Father's hands.

I believe that in time scientists will discover, as I have, that so many cancer victims have harbored a grudge of long standing against a person.

One, whom I knew, happened to be a woman who detested her daughter-in-law to such a degree that the daughter-in-law felt uncomfortable in her presence. I asked her one day, after the daughter-in-law had left, why she felt so antagonistic toward this girl. She told me it was because she felt the girl had taken her boy from her. The girl made a wonderful wife and mother, and I am afraid I was not too sympathetic with the mother-in-law.

The mother-in-law was a very religious woman, and she became quite irritated with me when I told her that until she released this animosity toward her daughter-in-law there would be no chance of her ever recovering from cancer. In fact, she did not talk to me for about a week or two.

Then she became very ill. She called me over and told me that I had been right, but she was too stubborn to admit it. She said that her son's wife was not the girl that she had wanted him to marry, and she had nurtured a grudge within her. If the girl was nice to her, she accused her of having an ulterior motive. If the girl did stand up for her rights, then she had a story to tell her son that his wife was treating her cruelly.

This woman became so very ill that, knowing my husband is also a hypnotist, she called him in and asked him if he could possibly help her. With the consent of the woman's doctor and her husband, Mr. Lauer regressed her to a very happy time in her life. The woman felt no pain whatsoever and she passed away with a smile on her lips, while under hypnosis.

A friend of mine who was very dear to me also developed cancer and I told her very frankly that she must have some begrudging thought in her mind about someone. Usually people get very angry when I tell them this, and if you who are reading this happen to have cancer, you may be angry, too. But until you get that thought out of your mind, you see, you are actually helping that cancer eat away the very tissues of your body. This friend of mine finally admitted that she was very angry with her mother, because her mother had been so unreasonable with her all of her life. Instead of expressing her displeasure, she had kept this inside of her. I begged her to talk to her mother without, of course, being disrespectful. I urged her to explain to her mother the feeling that she had within her all these years.

My friend did talk to her mother, then went ahead with a cancer operation. Today she is well and happy, and she has said that since she released the hatred from her mind, she and her mother are very dear to each other. Her mother told her that she had not meant to be cruel, but she felt that she had done the right thing at that particular time.

I have talked to many, many people who have had cancer, and in each and every case, the person has admitted that he nurtures a grudge against someone. I am convinced that if one harbors hatred, it becomes a corrosive, self-consuming acid.

When you have once put the Golden Magic Circle around you, you will feel entirely different from what you have ever felt before. You will almost feel a "presence." Things that once bothered you and caused you to be very concerned suddenly will not be quite as important as they were before you had the Golden Magic Circle around you. Don't be surprised if people notice a change in your personality.Those sensitives who are able to distinguish your aura will now see a difference from what they saw before. Your dynamic thought atmosphere will be radiant. You will possess a certain magnetism and graciousness. There will be a pronounced air of truth, goodness, and peace that you have never noticed before. You can select anything you want in this life. If you just visualize what you want and fix it firmly enough in your mind, it will come to pass. Keep this in mind as you draw your Golden Magic Circle around you.

And now we come to the most important part of this chapter. By this time your mind should be ready to accept what I am going to tell you, and this is the actual ritual.

To make your Golden Magic Circle, visualize a golden circle, quite a large one, completely surrounding you. This alone brings you much good. This circle shall never leave you. If you happen to be in danger, upset, or discouraged, you should just remember that your Magic Circle is completely surrounding you. Since this Magic Circle is of God, you know it is good. The moment you have pictured your Golden Magic Circle around your body, spread your arms and visualize that area as being completely filled with golden light, your own mental and spiritual kingdom. You can now be queen or king in this particular area, as you become oriented to this Magic Circle.

Visualize now a golden line of infinity, going from the top of your head to God, as your lifeline goes to God as a source of supply, rather than to the world. Visualize this lifeline holding you aloft when you are tired, feeling old, or discouraged. you will instantly notice that your head goes up, your spine stiffens. You will be erect so long as the Magic Circle cord is tight. You pull upward against the forces of earth's gravity. You have the Magic Circle if you have the ability to pull against the earth's gravity.

Now visualize another line going from your diaphragm, or waist, to the horizon. This is the other lifeline which ties you to God's infinity. As you breathe deeply of the golden elixir that surrounds you in your Magic Circle, you will be sustained and supported. You may feel at this moment that His presence is all around you. You will never feel alone again, because always beside you in your own Magic Circle is this invisible presence of God. You will know that things will be different from this moment on. Whenever you are upset, give a little tug to your lifeline, and you will receive help almost instantaneously, or something will come to you that will tell you what to do and what to say in this particular instance. Opportunities may present themselves at this time which will be very astonishing to you. You should let the quality of your soul rise above petty annoyances, as they can only affect the physical you: they can never destroy the immortal, or divine, part of you which is your soul.

Troubles may arise and you may become upset and tempted to let go. That is the time to pull up on the invisible cord which ties you to God's line, to raise your thoughts, to lift up your eyes to Heaven and, instead of being limited to this earth's horizon, breathe deeply and inhale the breath of God.

A baby cries out and proclaims its entrance into the world. This infusion of the breath of life is God's Magic Circle. A child has faith in its parents. This is the kind of childlike faith you must have in God. You should feel that your hand is placed in His, and then you can fear no evil.

I also wish to include in this chapter a ritual that was part of the mystic rites in the temple of Isis and Osiris. It was believed that the human psychic nerve centers could be stimulated to produce effects on the body and brain. For this purpose, a rite or invocation was indulged, which has been translated loosely in English as follows:

Oh, eternal flame, symbol of purity and creative life, I invoke the flood of thy creative power to now make manifest the conditions described in the worlds now being consigned to the living flame. The word is now made flesh, and I confide the hidden, secret desires of my mind, heart, and soul to the creative spirit of the universe. All obstacles are now being removed; dust to dust, ashes to ashes; the invisible spirit released by these creative words now assumes individual identity and finds its fulfillment.

The words and thoughts now released from the burden of the physical and material world now reach the subjective mind of the universe and become objectified. Flame, creative life, return to the source of thy origin, and manifest as creative spirit that which is entrusted to thee. I express faith in the power that rules time and space, that these conditions will be fulfilled. It is done, and I give thanks, O eternal spirit, ruler of the universe!

This invocation is implemented by writing on a piece of paper your desires and wishes, and then setting fire to them in a little dish, or before an altar with two lighted candles. As you watch the paper burn, recite the invocation with feeling and faith. As the paper dissolves to ashes, the obstacles dissolve and eternal spirit works in the invisible to manifest the condition you ask. Do *not* use this invocation for harm, or to destroy another, for it will only serve to destroy you.

I have included the above invocation for those who may wish to utilize it, but I do not think it is necessary if you follow all the instructions for your Magic Circle.

By drawing a complete circle in the space we have purposely left below, writing in it the things you want, then laying it aside and relying completely on your Magic Circle, you will later be able to check off each item as having manifested itself in your life.

CIRCLE HERE:

Many people, instead of writing in the circle that I have mentioned above, prefer to put actual pictures in the circle. For instance, if you want a certain type of house, look in a magazine and find a picture of that type of house to place within your circle.

Many years ago I was very anxious to have a daughter. After the birth of my son, the doctor insisted that I should think twice before having another child. Yet I knew that I wanted a daughter very badly. So I cut a picture of a very beautiful little girl out of a magazine and placed it within the circle. If you could have seen my daughter when she was born you would have agreed that she was almost an exact replica of the child in the photo. This is something that I can prove. Therefore, I would suggest to women who may have their eyes on a young man to marry, be certain that he is the man you want, because once you have that person in your life, it is not so easy to walk away from him. That is why I tell young people not to be impulsive, to know the person they marry; by so doing, they can save themselves many tears.

But I know also that by drawing this circle and placing the desired items within its boundaries, whether by writing or by picture, the day will come that you can check off each item as having been manifested in your life. You will be able to realize that your own intuition grows stronger each day. There is absolutely nothing that you cannot have in this life if you use the right method to obtain it. But do not think that you can mis-use the Golden Magic Circle in any way. It just cannot be done without the law of retribution balancing the scale.

Notes

Notes

Chapter Two

Attaining Life's Goals
Through Visualization

The instructions contained in this chapter have helped thousands of my clients obtain that which seemed impossible. Hundreds have mentioned the "almost magical powers" of visualization. But once one has mastered the psychic formulas, he will learn that attaining one's goals through visualization is really quite a simple matter.

THERE ARE THREE STEPS in visualization:
   1. Selection
   2. Visualization
   3. Gratitude

If you have previously tried visualization without success, you may have omitted one of the above steps. Visualization cannot become reality until all the steps have been fulfilled. One must have completeness of procedure.

Exactness of purpose and selection of what one wants is important. This is not to be confused with wishful thinking or daydreaming, because I can tell you right now that if you daydream, you will get nowhere. Why? I believe I shall leave that question for you to answer, and you should be able to have that answer by the time you have finished reading this chapter.

Many people have asked me, "Is it wrong to ask for, or desire, wealth?" No, I do not think so. However, should you receive all you have petitioned for, you should definitely not misuse what has been granted you. It is the *love* of money which the Bible warns us against, not the possession of it.

The same can be applied to health—your fear of illness may often produce disease. Why not change your fear into faith, knowing that you can just as well be healthy, successful, and happy, instead of being miserable, poor, and unhappy?

These things, I assure you, have to be cultivated in your mind before they can happen. Would you plant a seed, then in a week's time become impatient and uproot the seed to see if it were growing? Of course not! But why wouldn't you? Because you *know* that the seed will grow. Yet sometimes you do not have equal faith in the things you desire actually becoming reality.

Our minds must be trained to be ready to put aside fear and disbelief. As I have stated before, and I can say this truthfully, there is nothing I have wanted that had not come to me *exactly* as I wanted it, with no variations or change of any kind. *It came exactly as I had it in mind!*

Incredible? Not at all! There is nothing supernatural about it, nothing mysterious. But when something like this does occur to me, I send a very grateful prayer to the Infinite God. It takes only a moment to offer thanks, yet so many people fail to express their gratitude.

I often say to people, "You now have acquired something you selected and visualized. Haven't you forgotten something?"

They usually answer, "I can't imagine what I've forgotten."

At this point, they are in for a session with me on the importance of being grateful. Often I will say to them: "When you wanted these things, you devoted many hours to hoping, selecting, and thinking how wonderful it would be when this or that took place, yet it only takes a second to be grateful!"

"Father, I thank Thee that Thou hast heard me, and I *know* Thou hearest me always," is a favorite prayer of gratitude that I use.

But, I often reverse the procedure and give thanks *before* I receive what I want!

People say, "But you're thanking ahead of time; how can you be so sure?"

My answer to that is, "You try it sometime, then you'll know why I do this." I am so positive that what I have asked for will take place that I give thanks ahead of time.

I can almost hear you saying, "Surely you must have wanted *some* things that weren't for your own good."

Yes, that is true, but I could not blame anyone but myself for that, because you see, the law, which is immutable, works for good or bad. This is a fact which many find difficult to believe, but that is why, in metaphysics, you see the words "Universal

Mind." The Bible says, "The rain falls on the just and the unjust." In other words, the Universal Mind works according to law.

Therefore, I always warn everyone, be certain that what you visualize is really what you want, for you will surely receive it!

Have you ever noticed the trend of thought of a man who is in poor financial circumstances? The chances are that you will hear him say, "We never have anything, we're always poor. Wonder why so-and-so is so well off? I work hard and he does only half as much, and yet, look how he prospers!"

In a sense, this person *selects* being poor, inasmuch as he is always proclaiming he is; while the wealthier man is busy thinking of how he will react when he reaches a goal and is constantly looking ahead.

I should like to point out another example. A restaurant that is prosperous always sets the tables ahead of the dinner hour. Have you ever really thought about that? The waitresses have every place set, never for one moment doubting that they will be filled.

Can you see what I am trying to convey to you? One might say, if he were to observe this in a critical manner, "My, that restaurant proprietor must be sure he will have that many customers coming in today."

But let us look in on a not-so-prosperous restaurant, and what do we see? No prepared plates, no waitresses waiting ahead at their various stations. The result? Very few customers.

You should never envy anyone who is prosperous, because he usually deserves what he possesses. I hear you say, "I know many who prospered through underhanded methods." Again, the Universal Mind gives out what the person desires, concentrates on, and finally achieves. If someone who is prosperous has become dishonest, he will not enjoy his prosperity for very long. This immutable law takes care of that, so it should be no concern of yours. Your concern should be in getting what you want without being dishonest!

I have waited until this point to tell you how to visualize. Unless you can do this as I outline it (and at first you may think that it is indeed a strange way of achieving a goal), it will never work. Try it and see for yourself! Are you ready?

Let us say that you are really in need of money. Visualize as much money as you want or need. How would you act if you had that money? You definitely would have no fear of meeting your debts, would you? You would see yourself paying the bills, acting as if you had all you needed, buying things for those whom you love and above all, being grateful for the material symbol you have received.

Remember, and this is most important: one should never *love* money, but one should be extremely grateful for being enabled to take care of obligations.

Perhaps you are worried over a health problem. Pretend that you were told at one time that you had an incurable disease, and then, later, the doctor called and said to you, "I made a mistake. I had the wrong chart." Immediately you would be very elated, and you would feel very healthy, because the possibility of being incurably ill has been removed.

If you are unhappy, think how you would feel if the person causing this unhappiness were to suddenly tell you that he had not meant to cause you pain. You would once again feel very happy, wouldn't you?

You must desire and act as if the condition you want were actually now present. And, as I have stressed, you must give thanks for the realization of your desires before the deed has truly been accomplished.

You can affirm and daydream all day and achieve no results. I have letters in my files saying, "I affirmed that my health would be better and it's worse." I have then attempted to show these people where they were in error: they did not *act* as if they were better!

If a person were to say, "I'm better," but not wholeheartedly believe it, or desire it hard enough, or visualize how he would feel if he were no longer ill, and if he were afraid to give thanks for something which, as yet, he had not received, his condition would not improve.

My faith has been strong since I was a child. In Sunday School the teacher would say, "How many of you have had your prayers answered?" Invariably, my hand would go up.

One day the Sunday School teacher said to me, "Honestly, Dorothy, are all your prayers really answered? I have noticed that you always have something to report."

On another Sunday she said, "Since Dorothy has such good results, maybe we'd better ask her what she says and find out how she prays."

Just as if it were yesterday, I remember saying, "Well, I just say, 'Thank you God, for whatever I ask for.' "

The Bible says, "Ask, believing you shall receive, and you shall." To this day I still am answering my Sunday School teacher's question. I cannot understand anyone not having sufficient faith in God to the extent of truly believing.

There is no such thing as being lucky, nor, as I say throughout this book, is there anything supernatural about achieving success. People like to believe that there are such things, but I have had too much experience in the past to accept that theory.

With visualization you can see in your mind's eye that which you want to be. Believe me, if you want something that isn't for your own good, you'll get that, too! So, be careful!

You may say, "Why should anything bad come to me?" The law does not discriminate, or judge your requests; it will simply give you what you ask.

You may say, "If this particular thing weren't good for me, why did God let it happen?" I do not think we should blame God for anything bad that comes to us. A negative situation occurs because somewhere along the path that is what we visualized. Until this is proved to you as a fact, though, you will go on wondering why negative things happen to you.

On one occasion, a woman wrote to me saying, "I insist that this man marry me. I know he doesn't love me but I love him and, in time, he will return my love." It is my belief, however, that it is very wrong to marry someone who does not truly love you. Love is something that very definitely cannot be forced.

I advised her that if this man really loved her, he would tell her so, whereupon she again wrote and said, "Well, he never actually said he cared, but I know he does."

After a year had elapsed, this same woman wrote to me again. This time she said, "I only wish I had listened to you. The man I told you about hasn't yet said he loves me. He is cold and indifferent and now I want to visualize him *out* of my life."

If this woman had faced facts and not imagined things, she would have saved herself a lot of misery. Evidently she did eventually visualize the man out of her life. She assured me that she certainly had learned a lesson, namely, not to visualize anything of which she was not sure.

Now, I feel certain that you can answer the question presented in the first part of this chapter. Wishful thinking will never achieve goals, because with only your daydreams, you have nothing concrete upon which to build.

Also, and I make this clear in all my chapters, *you must not visualize harm to any other person.* Harming someone else will never bring true happiness. Once we realize the profound truth that the Universal Mind plays no favorites, we will know what we must do. For instance, if you think thoughts of hatred or revenge, someone who also is thinking these same thoughts will be tuned in and receive this consciousness. When you change your thoughts to good, you tune in to someone who thinks accordingly.

If, for instance, you need money, someone who can supply this need will receive your thoughts and be attracted to you, or he will be put in your life to help you. A businessman who may need a certain order may send out thoughts that transmit his wants. Someone capable of supplying that particular need will in turn contact him, because the thoughts were received.

I have had people say, "Now, how can so-and-so, who doesn't know me, possibly give me business that I need?" Well, you, who sends out this strong thought, and the person who needs the work done are on the same wavelength, so to speak.

It is very true that minds, thinking alike, are attracted to each other. You may sit back and wonder, "Why doesn't everyone do this?" The fact is, everyone does not know how to accomplish visualization. Once you get the idea of this psychic law, you will never again want for anything!

Believe me, there are no superbeings; all souls are created equal, but some have found the way to attract those things which they need. I am sure that by this time you have come to the conclusion that if the selection, visualization, and gratitude are present, you simply cannot lose.

Many times businessmen have asked me, "How can I attract more business my way?" In answer to this question, I give them the formula for visualization and, inevitably, soon they write back, saying, "It worked!"

I ask that you look back upon your life a little. Have you ever felt upset over something of a trivial nature? I would be willing to wager that not too long a period of time elapsed before you met someone who talked of nothing *but* trivialities. You see, your tuning power was on trivia, and someone, thinking along these same lines, was immediately drawn to you.

Perhaps you changed your way of thinking when different people came into your life, and you realized that you were not interested in providing companionship for the person who talked only of trivialities. It was at this point, you will recall, that Mr. Trivia vanished from your life!

Yes, my friend, it is as simple as that! No matter what it is, whether it is money, love, or happiness you want, send out strong vibrations, and someone who can meet those very needs will be attracted to you.

There may be times when you look back, saying, "It's strange how I met that person," yet this person was meant to be in your life. Perhaps he helped you financially, brought you happiness or love, or whatever it was that you needed.

I can only stress over and over, *watch your thoughts!* For instance, if you want to be very successful, look the part, act the part, and before long you will meet the very people who are members of the category to which you would like to belong.

I only wish that I could talk to each and every one of you personally and show you how easily visualization may be accomplished. Through the medium of this book, it is my sincere hope that I am reaching you as closely as though you were right here beside me.

Please follow my instructions implicitly, won't you? I urge you not to rush through this book; instead, read each and every paragraph thoroughly, and I am certain that you will absorb what I am attempting to convey to you. If you were to rush through these chapters without completely understanding them, you would be liable to say, "Oh, it may work for her, but it doesn't work for me!" You see, before you tried you would already be saying that visualization does not work!

For example, let us study an unsuccessful man. He wishes he could be successful and stay in business. While he is wishfully thinking of his goals, the bold, daring man, who does not underestimate his ability, reaches the goal that the poor, wishful thinker hopes faintly to reach.

A simple rule to keep in mind is this: All I have to do is to visualize the experiences I wish to have in this life and, in this way, I can control my own future.

I am positive that you can shape your own destiny and life, but because it is so easy, it appears hard. I am hoping that one day you will say, "At last I have found out, Dorothy, that what you say is true. By my own thoughts, I shape my destiny. That to which I give my undivided attention reveals itself as truly as it is stated."

If you have the ability to be a writer, by all means use it. If you have the ability to be a speaker, you definitely should not hesitate to speak before the public. Become an expert in whatever you are gifted in: do not do anything halfway!

No doubt you have heard of many miraculous healings which have taken place. Healing is really a loosening of congestion. Congestion is congealed life. When the congestion is gone, out flows miraculous healing. Churches provide beautiful music to arouse the emotions. The leaders of churches are very intelligent, learned people, and they know that the emotional fire that burns within releases the condition that causes illness. Here is the secret of miraculous healing. By "emotion" I do not mean to imply wild or hysterical excitement; I mean only a conviction of healing so deep that it hastens the curative processes.

I do not think that anyone should take credit for healing another person, because, truly, Universal Mind does the healing *through* the one who has the conviction that he is healed. It is the natural law that accomplishes healings.

When you are grieving over something, have you noticed that nothing tastes good, and no mater how you exercise, you seem to be devitalized? I was acquainted with someone who always felt ill when faced with responsibility. When she was relieved of the responsibility, she would be her old self again, feeling positively wonderful.

If you are historically minded, you are aware of the fact that the "king's touch," as it was called, resulted in many healings. Why? Because the laws of the mind are universal and can be made to work by anyone.

Have you ever heard the story about the man who was always very healthy? One day his friends decided to try to upset him, each one saying to him, "My, you look bad today. Don't you feel well?" By the end of the day he was a very sick man. The thoughts of poor health became so deeply imbedded in his mind that he actually became quite ill.

When my children first entered school, I checked the long list of children's diseases on their health cards and wrote the word "No" on back of each one of them. The doctor was quite surprised. I told him that the only thing they had ever had was a very slight case of measles. Their records remain the same today—not one disease has been marked. We have never talked illness, felt illness, or been unduly concerned when around ill people. I do not mean to imply that I do not believe in medical doctors. On the contrary, I have the utmost admiration and respect for them. By all means, consult your doctor if you are ill. Common sense must be used in connection with everything, and this applies even to this wonderful subject that can do so much for you.

I have often been asked if I smoke cigarettes. No, I do not. I do not need whatever it is that they seem to supply to other people. In my consciousness, there just are not any cigarettes! Do you see how it works? Neither am I a vegetarian, much to the dismay of several people who write me. I feel people should live as they wish, and they will then attract the kind of people who are in accord with their thinking! WATCH AND SEE!

Through emotion, liquefy that which you wish healed. The fervent emotion (strong, but not hysterical or wild) will cause the liquefying process to take place, and your strong conviction will produce the results of healing.

Have you ever noticed that when a new disease is discovered and its symptoms appear in the newspapers, very soon you will hear of more people reporting these same symptoms? The thought of the disease became so strong in their minds that the attraction took place.

Notice how merchandise is sold. The trade name that is uppermost in your mind when you buy an article was put there through advertising. The advertising men know the power of attraction and have learned how to place an idea, thought, or picture in the subconscious.

How many people exercise their minds? By exercising your mind, you will find new releases that will surprise you. First, relax, let every muscle become limp, then tense completely. Relax and tense about five times, and you will be amazed at how stimulated you feel. Try this daily and you will definitely see a difference in your personality.

When confronted with a very serious problem, I again say that you should always remember that you must make God the first to be honored. If you are troubled, upset, or wondering about the outcome of anything, I suggest that you say: "The Spirit of the Lord goes before me and makes easy and successful my way." Do not doubt! Here again is the law in action—you are saying the way will be easy for you.

It is only for you to take command of your life and shape it accordingly. For anyone to say, "It is the will of God that I'm poor, ill, and so on," is very wrong. Yet many people believe this, so they continue on their way, believing their misery is God's will. That I shall never believe.

I am going to say something here that I hope you will accept and understand: sometimes people are just too lazy to exert themselves, so making the "will of God" responsible makes it easy for them to drift along, getting nowhere.

If we are to believe the Bible, how can we not also believe that "As your faith is, so shall it be to you." God will be to you just as you imagine Him to be. If you decide He is a stern judge, dealing out misfortune and misery, then that is what He will be to you. Change your concept of God to that of a deity who gives you abundant life, health, happiness, love, and see what a different God He appears to be.

Some readers may resent several things I have said here, yet I feel I must be honest in my teachings, and I hope you will accept these lessons in that attitude. I have tested everything I write, and I am so certain of every word that I would gladly put a guarantee on each exercise I give you.

Please, do not read this book once and then think, "Well, it *does* take effort," and put it aside. If you will change your concepts, THINGS WILL CHANGE FOR YOU!

It is not for you to say to the Universal Mind, "I want this *my* way." You may need several channels in order to get what you want out of life.

Words are most powerful. Let us say that you visualize the things you want, yet your words are different from what you visualize. If you have visualized that you are healthy and happy, but continue to tell your friends that you do not feel well, that you are utterly disgusted with life in general, and so on, you are counteracting the visualized picture with conflicting words.

Therefore, conditions may go from bad to worse, because the visualization is powerful, but your words are also a potent force.

The word is as powerful as thought. Combine the right word and visualization and you have the perfect combination to bring your goals and desires into your life.

You should also realize that consideration of your neighbor is very important. This does not mean that you have to love a neighbor whom you do not particularly care for as a friend, but you should hold a certain degree of deep inner conviction that you wish that person well. You cannot expect to visualize all good things for yourself and never once think of your neighbor. It only takes a second to send a blessing to the person who may be tired, who may be sorrowful, and you do not even have to tell them you are doing this. You will, however, notice added changes in their life that will make you smile secretly to yourself, because you have used this powerful law for them, wishing them well. When your own dear ones say something to hurt your feelings, instead of being angry with them, sit down quietly and send them a silent message, a blessing. This will work much faster than a telephone call or a telegram, because these thoughts are so quick to reach the individual that harmony has to take over. But if you harbor negative thoughts toward someone, you will find that they will cause you to be ill, unpleasantly depressed, and irritable.

You must come to the conclusion that your spoken words and your thoughts are the most important things that you can exercise in the right way.

A former acquaintance of mine had a very tasteless sense of humor. She was the type of a person who would call you on the phone and say that she had gone to the doctor and was told she had cancer. Unless you knew this person, you would naturally feel shocked and sorry for her. Then, a few days later, she would call up and tell you that she had been joking!

Now I wonder if you can tell me what happened to this particular person? You see, she had been putting that powerful word into effect. She had said that she had cancer so many times to so many people that she had placed this powerful thought not only in her own subconscious, but into the thoughts of her friends. The day came when she did have cancer. You can imagine the shock that was in her voice the day she called and said, "I'm really not joking, I do have cancer!"

I tried to be very understanding with her, but I did tell her that I had warned her so many times that the day would come when she would be like the boy who cried "Wolf!" No one answered when the wolf really was there.

That which she had thought had actually been brought upon her. While this woman never got over the shock of her condition, it did teach her a lesson. She was very careful from that day forward. She had learned that part of the lesson, but I am sorry to say, it was just a little too late. However, I should say that she later went out of her way many times so that she could help other people see the error of their ways. So you see, all was not lost.

Some of you may have heard of what is called "treasure mapping." In this method of visualization, one pastes various things he wants on cardboard, dates it, sets it aside, looking at it every once in a while, and checks off each item as it comes to him. The individual who favors "treasure mapping" is the type of person who needs a visual picture before him. With mental visualization, one needs only to close his eyes and picture the object or goal of his desire.

From time to time, people have written to tell me that perhaps they may be going against God's word or will if they were to use visualization. For those who need such reassurance, you will find that none of these techniques go against anyone's religious beliefs. I believe these techniques may all be found in the Bible, and you may refer to the many passages and references which I cite.

Usually when neighbors of mine become acquainted with me, they seem to be astonished that everything that I have in life are things I have wanted. I am so happy to sit down and talk with them, as I am to you as you read this chapter, and tell them that I am no chosen person. I am not one bit different from them. This good news is meant for everybody. At first, of course, they are very skeptical, and they glance at me with strange looks on their faces. Then, gradually, they come and tell me how each little thing they have visualized has occurred. To many people this may appear as magic, but remember, it is not. It is a tuning in of the Universal Mind.

You will find that visualization is going to work for you in so many wonderful ways that it will be very hard ever to go back to your old way of doing things. It will be almost as if you have your wishes at your fingertips. You will learn to select, rather than to visualize at random. You will be very careful what you visualize, because you know it will come to you.

With visualization you will find a deep, inner calm. You will be able to discern which of the things you desire will play a truly important part in your life. Many of these visualized ideals which you put into this thought-form will include other people. When you build a home, the first thing that is laid is the foundation, and that foundation has to be firm in order for it to be the home that you want it to be. That is exactly the way with visualization. First build the foundation, then the rest of the visualization, and suddenly you will find people asking you what is happening in your life. Even those people with whom you work at your place of employment will notice a difference. Those who have been grouchy and hard to get along with will find that they can no longer be irritable with you. It will be almost as if you carry an aura of peace around with you. People will be sensitive to this aura to such a degree that they will go out of their way to want to be your friend and to learn what the secret is that you possess. And you must always be willing to tell a person how to achieve visualization. It is so much better to guide a person, to wish him well, and tell him how to accomplish visualization, than it is to hold this force within yourself and not share it.

You may have many new people entering your life, because Universal Mind is at work and it will draw people into your environment so that you in turn may bring this idea to them. At first they may look at you in disbelief, but as visualization works, you need only go by the direct results. It is the same as in the old saying, "The proof of the pudding is in the eating." The proof of visualization is in the results you receive.

You will find, too, that if you help someone, he in turn will help another person. Never force these ideas on anyone. When they are ready to accept them, just as you are ready to accept them now, I am sure, they will be guided to this very book.

You will find that lost articles can be visualized and relocated. Sit down quietly—not frantically, wondering where the item is— and visualize in your mind's eye a blank space. Then open your mind to the Universal Mind, and the thought will come to you where that lost article is; and nine times out of ten, you will find it. If you visualize for a long period of time, and you receive an impression on your visualized thought pattern of a void, absolutely nothing, this means that the article has been permanently lost.

You must never visualize anyone becoming ill or passing away. This is something that I am very much against, and I never encourage anyone to do it. It is not right. If you ever attempt it, remember it can work, and the law of retribution will have to be paid back by you, perhaps by suffering the very thing that you caused that other person to go through. We are not put here to hurt other people, nor to judge them. We all have enough to do to take care of our own lives. If people do things that you do not think are quite right, stop and visualize them doing the right thing and they will be guided.

If you take blank pieces of paper, jot down what your visualization ideas are, and record the date next to them, I can guarantee that in the future you can write in the dates of their materializations. However, you must not put time limits on your visualizations. This again is a dictate of the Universal Mind. It is very powerful. If you throw a pebble into water, at first there is just a little round circle, then it ripples out bigger and bigger. It is the same with visualization.

I know that you will have success, because I have put the idea of visualization across to many thousands of people. I can truthfully say that only about one person out of every one hundred has failed to achieve results, and these people went into visualization with doubtful minds. These people had decreed that visualization would fail before they even tried it. So much is in your hands when you use this very valuable asset.

Many of you have become disappointed that you have not yet attained certain goals in your life. Even though you may have given up, those goals can be still reached. There is no such thing as not being able to do that which you set your mind to do. I feel that since I realize that my mind is there to use—at all times under my own will—I can do anything I so desire. I know it is quite a statement to make when I say that there has been *nothing* kept from me that I have wanted. So it may be with you. It may seem as if I am offering you a key to everything the world has to give—and I am! Visualization will work for you!

Chapter Three

How to Make Mental Telepathy Work for You

Telepathy is a subject that holds fascination for the majority of people, and it can be most interesting to try. Again, I give you the warning that it must be used correctly or not at all.

AS YOU PRACTICE mental telepathy, you will find that it is as if you have an invisible telephone constantly before you. I am sure that as you use telepathy, many people will be surprised to find themselves calling you, because they have received your mental message. Start out with little experiments rather than large ones. I am sorry to say that mental telepathy can be detrimental, but people of a higher consciousness cannot be attracted to do that which is not within them to do. No evil thoughts, no debased thoughts, no lustful thoughts can touch you unless you are on the same mental wave as a person who is sending those kinds of thoughts. You can prevent such thoughts from coming through; you can develop a control that can erase negative thoughts immediately.

Unfortunately, there are many people who would attempt to use telepathy in such a manner as to accomplish lustful acts and actually bring disaster to wonderful people. But remember you are surrounded by the Golden Magic Circle. This is one reason why I felt that this message must be written down in book form, so that you may choose that which you want in life. This is why we are given free will. We can be good; we can be bad; we can do the things we know we should do; and we can also neglect our responsibilities if we so desire.

Mental telepathy is a facet of metaphysics that is quite easy to demonstrate, and with the exercises I shall give you, you should have immediate results.

Should anyone feel that telepathy is simply a figment of the imagination, then, of course, to that person telepathy can never possibly become a reality.

To those of you who are interested in developing telepathic ability, I urge you to study with an open mind, refusing to allow prejudice to distort your experimentation. Telepathy means simply that one can, through the mind, make contact with another. You will be very surprised at the many things you will discover through the use of telepathy.

When you experiment with telepathy for the first time, you may find to your amazement that you soon hear from someone whom you have had in mind a great deal, almost as if they *knew* you wanted to hear from them. There will be times, though, when you may encounter a delay, but do not let this discourage you; the thought will have reached its destination if, at the time you sent the message, you felt a response.

How does one feel a telepathic response? You may experience a little tingle in your arm, or a feeling that your thought has reached its destination. I urge you, though, not to go into a trancelike state, nor to "imagine" that you feel this tingle. If it is there, you certainly will not have to imagine it—it will be real enough!

You will usually know, without a doubt, that the message has been received. You must learn to realize that time and space mean nothing. You must seek to develop a feeling of oneness with everyone.

When people write to me, I can actually feel their needs. Although it is impossible for me to meet these people personally, I am still able to know their problems and to answer them by giving my impressions.

Many times the impression will come to me that someone is in very difficult or unhappy circumstances. Instantly I will write to this particular person, giving them my advice with the hope that I can be helpful to them. Since this is done voluntarily on my part, people realize that I certainly have no monetary motive connected with my writing. In other words, there is no fee for this. I simply have an intense desire to help anyone whom I feel is very troubled. But I will not allow anyone to take advantage of me, either!

There are times when people write to me in what I consider to be a rather demanding manner, saying, "Write me! I need to know this or that!"

When this occurs, I simply cannot answer them, as they are trying to *force* me to do so. Force must never be used in connection with mental telepathy or any other occult ability.

Those people who are in tune with your feelings will immediately receive your message without the slightest bit of trouble. It seems as though an affinity exists between those who receive and those who send the messages.

I am definitely against anyone attempting to send a telepathic message that could harm others or cause them to be unhappy. Telepathy is such a wonderful talent and it certainly should not be misused.

True affinity leads to complete, true, and specific communication. The feeling is so strong that it is as if you were actually seeing the person with whom you are in rapport. You learn too not to try to contact anyone when you feel they desire privacy. As in any matter which affects two people, one does not force issues.

Telepathy is *not* mind reading. There is a difference that you will be able to see once you begin your experiments. I would intensely dislike having anyone feel that I could read his mind. So, by all means, do not confuse telepathy with mind reading.

In true telepathy, there is an attitude of awareness about you. Should someone be angry, you will feel the anger just as plainly as if he had spoken of it to you. At this time you might say, "I feel you are angry over something." Let it go at that, though.

If you have felt exceptionally well all day, and then, while in a group of people, you suddenly feel quite ill, you have received an indication that someone in the room is experiencing ill health. It is not necessary, however, for you to make a spectacle of yourself by asking, "Who feels ill in this room?" This would certainly be a wrong thing to do.

If you are with someone whom you feel is not telling the truth, you will definitely feel his deceitful attitude, just as you will experience a sense of calmness and quiet understanding when in the company of someone whom you like very much.

If, as a rule, you do not suffer from headaches, and then suddenly you have one, you can rest assured that someone around you has one also.

If you are aware of the fact that one person in particular would strenuously object to your sending him telepathic messages, by all means do respect his wishes.

There are those who become obsessed with a subject: I stress the point that you should never become so engrossed in ESP that you forget to live and to have a normal life. In other words, do not go overboard with the study of metaphysics! I have never permitted myself to become so absorbed in these subjects that I have excluded everything else. At a moment's notice, I can forget the world of ESP and all its phases if I am among people who are unaware of the fact that I am interested in such subjects.

Most people resent feeling that their thoughts may not be their own, that others can send messages to them or have the ability to actually read their minds. Do not misuse your telepathic ability! It is quite possible that someone might say to you, "If you can tell me my house number, I'll believe in your ability," or they might expect you to tell them the serial number on a bill. To me, this is no proof at all. However, if you were to tell someone that by being impulsive he could suffer a loss which could not be regained, I would consider this statement as being of real service to someone.

I feel, too, that it is very wrong to use telepathy in attempting to contact someone who has passed on. Telepathy should only be used if you are very sincere and have a real desire to help others.

As an experiment in telepathy, try this: Think of someone from whom you would like to hear, then visualize his calling. If this person were to call you, the first thing he would do would be to dial your number. Then what next: The phone would ring, so you must *hear* the phone ring in your mind, and here is where many make errors. Many people have written to me saying, "Never has anyone written that you have to visualize the actual action taking place." This is the point at which so many metaphysicians have failed to make their affirmations work. If they were to visualize the words as being an act, their affirmations would work like magic.

Getting back to our experiment, now that the phone has rung, what will happen next? Naturally, you will answer it. In your mind, *hear* his words as you know his particular way of speaking, his own special mannerisms on the phone. Once you have visualized this, do not keep the picture in your mind for hours. Release it, and the phone will ring! Unless these instructions are followed implicitly, however, you can picture someone calling you all day to no avail.

While visiting in Chicago, I learned that a very dear friend of mine had moved to Canada. I had an overwhelming desire to hear from this person so I sent her a telepathic message asking her to call me. By the way, this particular friend did not believe in anything of this nature.

My thoughts evidently hit this friend very plainly. As I released my message, I also sent my name via the telepathic impulse. After all, one can hardly call another and not reveal her identity. You see, every detail has to be perfect, just as if it were actually taking place.

Now, in addition to my desire to contact my friend, there was urgency, and a great deal of it, in back of the message which I sent. My friend had left home in anger and her mother had attempted suicide. No one knew where to reach her. After the police had failed to locate her, an appeal was made to me and I was asked to send the message, which I did, unhesitatingly.

The next day, believe it or not, my friend called Chicago and returned as soon as she could. Had she returned the call immediately upon receiving my message, she would have seen her mother again. However, since she had put off calling until the next day, her mother had died before her arrival.

Mental telepathy is like having a private telephone wire to anyone whom you wish to contact. I hesitate to write on many of its phases, because I know what misuse people could make of them. Before any of these chapters go to press, I shall offer a quiet prayer that the recipients will not misuse the contents.

To those of you who have used affirmations for years but without results, I urge you to try the method described here. Go through the procedure as if it had already taken place, only be very sure that you truly want such a thing to happen to you, because it definitely will, just as surely as the dawn comes each day!

I have often heard people say, "This happened just as I had imagined it." It was not imagination; it was mental telepathy at work. Look back upon your own life. Have not several things happened which were so exactly true to your desires that you have said, "I knew it! I knew it would happen!"

I urge you to be certain of what you want, because these affirmations can bring you anything you wish. Many metaphysicians have written to me saying, "I've used affirmations for years and nothing happened. The moment I did as you said, however, things began to happen."

If you want money, do not wishfully think, "I'd like to have money." Instead, in your mind, see the money already in your hand, picture yourself buying the thing you want, and already living in the consciousness that would be yours if you had this money. You could wish for money every day for years and still not possess it. However, the moment you actually feel the money around you, and see yourself in your mind purchasing the things you have desired, the money will be yours! But you must not defraud anyone to get it!

Often people have remarked to me, "Why does everything you've ever wanted come to you?" It is simply because I know these things will be mine; to me, they have already been granted. The Bible talks plainly about "having faith of things not seen." It is so simple that sometimes I become a little upset over the fact that people make such an issue of something that is so apparent. I know you will say, "Well, everything comes your way, no wonder you say that." Yes, that is true. Nothing has ever been denied me that I really and truly wanted. I realize that this is a pretty broad statement to make, yet it is the truth.

I have had some mighty astonishing demonstrations, and that is why I am very careful before I visualize anything in my life. If I am very sure I really want something, I know the immutable law will take over and I will have whatever I desire. Sometimes your goal may not materialize as soon as you would like, but you cannot force time!

When people say to me, "I just cannot make money," I reply with, "Well, of course you can't. Haven't you, just by those very words, set into motion the thing you *want?* You just said you cannot make money, so until you change your mind and know you can, you never will."

Try to feel that you are as well off as you would like to be. Right now I am counting my own blessings. Since there seems to be nothing I want at this time, I shall visualize for others.

Should you wish to become a "sending station," do this: Sit alone in a quiet room, shut out all other thoughts, and picture the person whom you wish to contact. In your mind's eye you will see him plainly and almost feel his very presence. In your mind, talk to that person just as if he were in the same room with you—not audibly, of course! Breathe deeply, for this gives needed power to the broadcasting station of the mind.

You may also send healing thoughts to those who are hospitalized, realizing that it is *not* you who heals, but your tuning in on the Infinite Mind, which can do all. If someone is bereaved, send him a thought that the Infinite will send its presence to his side.

If someone is endeavoring to stop a bad habit, picture the person hating the habit so much that he, of his own free will, will give it up.

Spend some time each day, not thinking of your own wishes and desires, but rather those of others. It takes only a little time to send a thought to someone who is ill, and it helps so much.

Never make an issue of the thoughts you send. Simply do it, and then forget it. We all know people who need help. However, do not say to them, "Well, this morning I sent you a thought on this or that."

In your mind, you can say that for a friend to continue a bad habit is hurting him, and you can, by sending him a telepathic message, be instrumental in increasing his will power to overcome his weakness. The impulse will not work, however, if you picture your friend in the act of engaging in his bad habit. You must picture him as having definitely given up the habit; in only this way will it be discontinued. The most vital point in this work is this: *You must actually see the desired condition and feel as if it were so!*

If you wish to see how a certain person reacts to you, make yourself a receiving station for someone's thoughts. Sit quietly and breathe slowly, but not too deeply. Picture in your mind that this particular person is before you, and you ask him point-blank, "What do you really think of me?" If you receive a very friendly and wonderful impulse, you will immediately become aware of the fact that he does like you. If you receive a feeling of deceit, that means he should be spoken to with caution. At this point, the voice of intuition is ready with an answer.

The Bible plainly states: "You shall decree a thing, and it shall come to pass." Many truths have been shown to us, but we have often misinterpreted them. This passage from the Bible should now have more meaning than ever: *You* shall decree a thing (meaning that you, yourself, should decree whatever it is you want out of life).

You may have heard the line from a poem, "I asked life for a penny and that is all I got." I wish that I could speak personally to each and every one of you. I know that I could convince you through my own demonstrations just how true these concepts are.

As you ask for yourself, remember others as well. Thought has wings, and the health, happiness, and good fortune you wish for others will indeed return to you, overflowing. A very old proverb says: "I helped my brother's boat across the stream, and lo, my own had reached the shore!"

Chapter Four

Discovering the Genie Within You

I am sure that you all have heard of Aladdin and his wonderful lamp. I don't expect you to be able to produce a lamp such as this, but what I am trying to bring to your mind is the fact that there is nothing impossible in your life. We each have within us the power of an Aladdin's lamp. Within each of us resides a "genie" awaiting our commands.

THERE IS NOTHING IMPOSSIBLE. I know that sounds like a very strong statement, but remember I have tested these techniques over a period of thirty-five years. Many times I have noticed that when people come to work for me, they look very skeptical. They just cannot believe that the things I speak of can occur, but little by little, subconsciously at first, and then later consciously, they begin to find these things in their own lives. They could hardly work for me and not have some of my abilities rub off on them.

Sometimes I smile to myself because there is often a period my employees go through that may, at first, bring some rather unpleasant conditions. Then, afterwards, I see the very same people having practically everything they want at their fingertips. But you see, they had not been using the genie within them as consciously as they should have for best results.

Some people need to have a visible means of attaining that which they desire. If you feel you need something like an Aladdin's lamp to rub, then go ahead and find some significant object. But you really do not need a physical crutch, because as you sit quietly and have this knowing power within you, you will find people coming into your life who will supply many of the things that you lack.

I am not going to tell you to sit quietly if you are a working person. You cannot sit home and not work. The genie within you would balk, and I would not blame him if he did. Once you have mastered the idea that you can bring into your own life and world the very things you want, you may rest assured that your genie will be working for you on the job or in your home.

There have been times that I have had things happen to me that people have labeled as "miracles." I do not consider them as such, because I know they came about because of my own great belief.

When doctors decreed that I would never have any more children after the birth of my son, I told them that I would have a very beautiful daughter. Five years later, I delivered a nine-pound baby girl. Even up to the time of labor, the doctors were skeptical in regard to the birth, and some warned that the delivery would take either her life or mine. But I had no fear.

Had I taken the word of the doctors and given up the idea of having another child, I probably never would have had one. But to me this child, this daughter who was born to me, had been as real on the day that the doctor told me I would never have another child as she was on the day that they placed her in my arms. I had presented the problem to the genie, the knower within us, and I knew that this was to be.

People go to church Sunday in, Sunday out, and they hear, "Ask and ye shall receive." They are told over and over again that their faith will bring them that which they desire. They hear this all their lives. They listen, but it just does not seem to penetrate their consciousness that much of the wisdom of the ages is written in the Bible. Regardless of the version you read, the Bible gives the promise of your faith bringing into your life that which you want.

If people would only stop and think, they would realize that they have everything at their command. Many years ago, one of my clients told me, "Dorothy, I can't get anywhere just sitting here thinking that everything is at my command. I am going to go to an antique shop, and I am going to find a lamp that looks like Aladdin's lamp if I have to look from here to the end of the earth."

Strangely enough, she did find a lamp that looked exactly like the familiar Aladdin's lamp. She was very happy with that lamp. She came home and shined it up beautifully until it glowed. She put it in a very conspicuous place in her living room and everyone who entered the room commented on her Aladdin lamp.

After she became adept at practicing the techniques I gave her, she came to realize that she did not really need her "magic" lamp. She kept the lamp in the parlor, however, because it was what had prompted her faith into realizing that the power was within her.

She admitted to me that many times while she sat there rubbing that lamp with a little blue felt—no ordinary cloth was used because it did not seem fitting—she would think to herself, "I must have this; I must have that. So be it." She arrived at the point where she would end each request with "So be it," which, strangely enough, is a pronouncement that many mystics use, because when one says, "So be it," it is as if one has declared, "It is done." This is mystical in the effect that it has.

Everything began to come her way. Everything, no matter what it was! She had found a wonderful mate, she had a beautiful car, beautiful home, and many times she would write to me and say, "I feel very guilty that I know this and I can't tell people about it, because most of them would look at me and think there was something wrong with me—just as I did when you told me about this, Dorothy."

One day the genie within me seemed to prompt me to walk down a certain street. Yet the street was too far from my home to walk there comfortably, and I do not drive. My neighbors were all out, and I thought, well, if I am supposed to travel to that location, the way will be shown for me to go.

A man whom I had telephoned three or four weeks previous to this date suddenly decided to come to give me an estimate on some work I had wanted done in my home. This man had never had any intention of coming when I called him nearly a month before—why should he come on that day?

When he arrived at our home he explained that he had felt as if his phone had rung and he received an impression of my voice. "I must go see what work Mrs. Lauer wants done," he thought, "but I have to go right now."

I said, "Well, that's fine." I did not go into detail with him, as I did not feel he would understand what I was talking about.

"Before you give me the estimate," I said, "would you kindly drive me…" and I gave him the name of the street.

He was very obliging. I knew that I had to go to this particular street, which was about ten to fifteen blocks from my home.

I felt that what I would see would have something to do with my daughter, and as we drove down the street, I saw my daughter with three other teenagers, their arms all around each other, laughing and being very gay. Evidently they had played hooky from school and were going to a malt shop.

You can imagine the astonishment on my daughter's face when she saw her mother riding down the street in a car with a strange man, then stopping and telling her to get into the car. She looked so flabbergasted! Although she had seen many psychic demonstrations before, she just could not believe it. However, that girl never played hooky from school from that day on, you can rest assured of that!

I had received an inspiration to go to a specific location. I did not sit down and ask the genie within me how I was going to get there. When I released that initial thought, I knew from that moment on that it would reach somebody, and it did.

There have been times when I have gone to events at which there are door prizes. Once someone had, oh, I think it was a $10 gold piece. I was not too interested in having this gold piece, but I thought I would try the genie within me on the prize. Sure enough, they picked my ticket out of the fish bowl in which they kept all the names.

I mention this so you may see that from a $10 gold piece to going somewhere that would prevent my daughter from playing hooky, the genie within works in a most strange and wonderful manner.

This is such a powerful intelligence within you; yet it is apart from you as a human being.

You have to be extremely careful in regard to certain people whom you may meet along life's pathway, who, knowing that you have this faith, may want you to use this force for them in the most unscrupulous ways. If you knowingly take advantage of someone, you yourself will lose twice as much as that which you have cost another. You must realize that you need to have your consciousness on a high plane. You cannot use this power with debased thoughts. You cannot use this force to hurt others.

Ever since I was a little girl, I have used ESP. My mother often said to me, "No matter what you want, Dorothy, you have it. It's almost as if paths were open to you in such a manner that you always achieve your wishes." And I would reply, "Well,

Mother, everyone can do this. I just don't know why you grownups don't use it."

I do not use the genie within me just for my own self. If I know that a person is a good person, who does not want to hurt anyone else, I am more than happy to help him with ESP until he himself can take over and do it on his own. I have had the most skeptical people come into my life and offer me fees for getting this or that for them. In spite of their skepticism, I have often obtained their goals in such a dramatic manner that they considered it magic. If it is magic, then I am not aware of it, and I certainly do not call it by that name. This power is within each of us.

The genie within us has often been accused of not working unless one uses certain words. Some metaphysicians say you must use only special ritualistic words in order to obtain results. No other words will do; they have to be these "magic" words. I do not believe that there are any perfect words, any "magic" words, because here again, you see, one would be placing restrictions on that genie within you, which is the very thing you should not do.

Let us say that you awaken some morning and feel exceptionally unhappy about the day. You are filled with foreboding. This usually means that something will happen that day that will possibly make you a little sorrowful. But if you rub your "magic lamp" or call upon the genie within you, you will gain some benefit from the day, regardless of what takes place. Somehow, some way, there will be a lesson learned.

There is an old saying that goes, "You have to relive an experience until you learn thoroughly not to make that same mistake again."

People who are very religious often ask me if I do not think that these techniques go against God's law. I definitely do not, because of the fact that one is using these psychic methods for good. If one were ever to use these mental formulas in the wrong manner, the law of retribution would take over, regardless of what religion you practiced or whether or not you attended any formal church at all.

I would like to quote from an article about me which appeared in the August 1961 issue of *Exploring the Unknown*. Called "The Amazing Dorothy Spence Lauer," the piece was written by Mr. Vance L. Milligan, a minister with an Ohio Baptist church. In the article Mr. Milligan tells how his mother questioned him about my work.

"Vance, I think the Bible speaks against such people as Mrs. Lauer. Remember in the Old Testament, in the book of Deuteronomy, chapter eighteen, verse eleven, which prohibited the people from consulting wizards, witches, and those who had familiar spirits [or trance mediums]. I want to know how you, as a minister of the Gospel, can go against the Bible, which is supposed to be your fundamental guide?"

"Good question, Mother," I [Milligan] answered. "Firstly, this scripture was binding only to the Hebrews of that time; these people were living under the Law; these people observed rituals, days, diet, and other activities that Jesus later considered unnecessary.

"As Christians, living under Grace, the New Testament is our guide. St. Paul, 1st Corinthians 12:4–11, states that clairvoyance, clairaudience, automatic speech, and other psychic phenomena are given each man for his profit or benefit—"

Mother interrupted, "Christ could do these things because he was part divine."

"Read John 14:12," I answered. "You will find that Christ said, '*Verily, verily, I say unto you, he that believeth in me, the works I do shall he do also; and greater works than these shall he do; because I go unto my father.*'

"Mrs. Lauer is not a tool of the devil. I strongly feel that God approves of people like Mrs. Lauer. She is a modern prophetess."

People have reported to me that they have received gifts, they have had many things brought to them so suddenly that it was hard for them to conceive that such power had been lying dormant within them all the time and they had never used it. They had not used this power because they had never learned how.

You do not have to have any formula to call upon the genie within you. All you have to do is to set forth the thought. I have told many people that the best way to do this is to picture your thoughts written with white letters on a blackboard. Then it is as if someone would take the blackboard and put it out of sight. The reason I say this is that once the idea is projected through the genie, you should relax and know that it is to be.

I know it will take a little while for you to get used to this idea, but once you have it, you will never lose it, and it will be something that you project as you meet people. People always seem to sense this power subconsciously, and they will often say to you, "Why is it that you always seem to have everything you want?" Let them ask, but do not force these techniques on anyone. Only if someone makes a direct request for knowledge should you explain this method to them.

There are many mystic schools which have had people write to them for a period of twenty to thirty years, and then, around the thirty-fifth year, I believe, they tell the long-suffering the very formula that I have told you here.

I am still in awe of this wonderful power within. I do not know why more people do not use it. They profess faith; they profess that they are living a good life; and perhaps in their estimation, they are. But they are allowing the very essence of themselves to lie dormant and, therefore, they are not getting out of life all they should.

Every time you condemn someone or judge them, you are also putting the genie within you into effect, so that you will bring into your own life the very experience for which you may be condemning another. Stop and think before you condemn a friend. Haven't you, at some time or other, been in the very position in which the person whom you are condemning finds himself? Nine times out of ten, you must answer "yes" to that question.

Remember that the genie within you is at your beck and call. Use it wisely, use it carefully, and there will be no need for any disappointment. You will also find that whenever something extra good is going to happen to you, you will feel a stillness, a quietness about you. This is the genie within you telling you to expect the good that will take place that particular day. Naturally, there may also be days when the genie will warn you that something of a negative nature might occur for which you must brace yourself. You must not look upon this as bad news, because you will be prepared to handle whatever situation you are faced with in the most extraordinary manner. Here, too, you will be putting into use the very faith that I have been telling you about throughout this book.

Chapter Five

Controlling Your Intuition

The Thorndyke-Barnhart Comprehensive Desk Dictionary *states that intuition is "Perception of truth or facts without reasoning." I hope you will remember this definition. The moment you start reasoning, then it is no longer intuition. Many people who have wanted to study intuition have begun reasoning at the same time, rather than relying solely upon intuition.*

It took me many years to come to the conclusion that if I was reasoning, then I was not letting intuition have full sway. This is one of the stumbling blocks that I think is a little difficult to overcome: one must not reason with intuition.

Intuition, of course, is spontaneous. Before I came to the conclusion that intuition was so very accurate, I would begin reasoning. Finally, however, I realized that when I began to reason, I was not so certain that intuition was altogether right. If I am successful in showing you how to use intuition correctly, you will have no further doubt in your mind.

On many occasions I have been asked, "Just how do you tell the difference between impulse and intuition?" First, intuition is something you can be sure of, but impulse, never!

Intuition is like a knowledge within yourself which leaves no doubts. Intuition, as with all real truths, works only for good. Impulse, on the other hand, can be either for good or bad. Impulse emerges from the lower self, whereas intuition comes from obeying the voice within.

With intuition, you will find that there is an awareness of feeling: "This is the right course to take." Impulse is not like that at all. With impulse, you feel a restlessness that urges you on; yet even when that impulse is obeyed, the restlessness still remains.

Intuition does not work this way at all. You have a feeling of being sure and calm and that you *know* the result. If you learn to control impulse by listening to the voice of intuition, you will rarely go wrong.

There are many who have studied intuition and impulse for years yet still do not quite understand the difference. The only way this distinction can be learned is by testing and testing until you finally know that the voice of intuition varies a great deal from that of impulse.

I assure you that you will definitely get results from any of the exercises described here. Try this experiment: Think of someone who is a long distance from you and then ask yourself, "Shall I call this person long distance?" (Keep someone in mind who is far enough away that it would necessitate quite an outlay of money for the call.) Now will come the thought, "Would this call be important enough to put this amount of money into it?" At this point, you will probably have an overwhelming desire to talk to this particular person. Here is where *impulse* will attempt to overcome *intuition*. Intuition will tell you the right thing to do. Should you now have a little feeling of doubt, do not make the call! Impulse will now take over, urging you to make this call regardless of cost. For some reason, though, you do not seem to have the same assured feeling of *knowing* that you have with intuition; this, believe me, takes practice.

As another experiment, try this: When you receive a letter, you may think to yourself, and without reasoning, of course, "I wonder if this contains good news or bad?" Then, remembering your first impression, open the letter to see if you are right. I would be willing to gamble that nine times out of ten, providing your intuition is in any way developed, you will be correct.

Supposing your telephone rings. Before answering it, say quickly to yourself, "I wonder who is calling me," and, once again, the first impression that comes to your mind will be the correct one.

Now, of course, we have to be sensible. We can not expect this faculty or ability to be trained overnight! We will doubtlessly make mistakes. There will be times when you may say, "Oh, I don't think there is anything to it. This was completely wrong!" When this happens, though, do not blame intuition. It is quite possible that you had too many things on your mind at the time, or that you were not depending entirely on intuition. This, of course, is logical in daily living, but when it comes to anything of an occult nature, you will discover that in almost every phase it is a *knowing* within you, which, to some, is an unexplainable mystery.

As we go on in our studies, we discover many things in life that at one time appeared to be of a mystifying nature. Do you know that the brain cells actually grow and expand when you keep them active? The body organs respond to mental stimulation.

Science also recognizes the fact that when people start to grow old, when they no longer study or develop their minds, they begin slowly to deteriorate. You must keep busy studying new things daily. Try to keep up to date on world affairs, and by all means have pleasant dreams for the future. Keeping the brain cells alive and active is indeed very important.

Use daily suggestions to the subconscious mind, and its wisdom will help you to grow and expand. Each day you will grow stronger in your ability to recognize the difference between impulse and intuition.

Often, before I was as certain as I am now of the difference between impulse and intuition, I would think to myself, "I feel as if I may hear something that could cause me tears if I go to this particular place." And sure enough, if I did go, I would hear something that made me feel sad.

Rarely do I give in to impulse, as I am now thoroughly aware of the restless feeling which accompanies it. Often I have thought, "Don't go to the store now or you'll miss an important call." Need I mention that I *did* receive an important call? The calm feeling associated with intuition is indication enough, as far as I am concerned, of how one should be guided.

I think the time will eventually come when people's minds will be so thoroughly developed that everyone will be able to rely upon intuition. Of course, here again all mystics will tell you that the voice of intuition is your oneness with the infinite, and it will indeed be a wonderful day when people learn to rely upon this extraordinary gift we all possess.

In truth, the great promise that was made so many years ago will be fulfilled: "Every knee shall bend." You see, until people realize there is only one Source, and none other, all men will have to learn the hard way.

People simply do not want to listen to intuition; it is so much easier to follow impulse. Through a daily contacting of the spiritual side of yourself, you will in time overcome the lower self, and this will definitely enable you to cross the bridge between intuition and impulse.

An unfolding of the intuitive mind to guide one's self-realization comes through identification with the object. If you will refer to Matthew 7:7, you will find the well-known words with which most of us are acquainted: "Ask, and it shall be given you; seek and ye shall find; knock, and it shall be opened unto you."

Take the first letters of the above mentioned admonitions, "ask," "seek," and "knock." Spell these out and what does it say? A-S-K—ASK!

Through the wonderful medium of prayer and through meditation, God will most certainly guide you by giving you wonderful thoughts and ideas which will come to your mind in the form of intuition. If you, through higher intuition within your superconscious mind, develop intuition to a point where it becomes supersensitive, you will indeed be very fortunate.

Along with intuition comes inspiration. Great artists and musicians are inspired, and in their particular gifts they can transmit whatever comes to them to others. Again, this is nothing more than "tuning in" and receiving.

When we tune in on a certain station on radio or television, we do not consider the station to be perfect until the sound is clear. This can, in a way, be compared with intuition. We must feel rested and calm, knowing "this is right." There is no other way to describe this, except as an "inner knowing."

If you follow intuition it can bring you much happiness. A great deal of practice as well as patience is required, however. Many times you may say, "I was certain this was intuition, yet it turned out wrong."

Intuition is never wrong. If you will check back, you will remember that you had a feeling of restlessness, which as I have stated before, is connected only with impulse. Once more let me repeat that there is absolutely no restlessness in connection with intuition!

Many of you who are just starting on the path of reliance upon intuition will be a little discouraged, I know. Yet in the chapters of this book I avoid technical terms, so that it will be easier for you to follow my instructions.

No chapter in this book was written until I was absolutely certain that I could pass on to you the techniques which have taken me thirty-five years to perfect.

No doubt you have often heard the advice "sleep on it," given perhaps in connection with a problem or something over which you were worried. Many times I have heard this suggestion, but when I was very young, I could not quite comprehend the meaning of it. However, as I grew older, I discovered how profound these words really were.

Morning will often bring a solution to a problem. Many great inventors have at times been puzzled as to how to proceed with the work in which they were engaged. Then they suddenly discovered that "sleeping on it" resulted in the answer.

Many authors say that they arise at two or three o'clock in the morning to jot down thoughts that have come to them. Many wonderful books have been written in the still watches of the night.

From Tibet comes the song "Celestial," a sacred rite of a Tibetan priest, who taught the following: First, there must be harmony and happiness; Second, this only comes about from finding God within; Third, release from the world's suffering comes through contemplation on the divine mystery; Fourth, hearts and minds must be raised in prayerful meditation. The Tibetans have a large prayer wheel to which they attach their prayers, and as the wheel turns thousands of prayers are sent heavenward.

The song "Celestial" reveals that Buddhists obtain their emancipation by means of their own minds, which are kept pure, transparent, and undefiled, thus enabling them to obtain the great enlightenment.

I would like to tell you about the Oriental lake exercise. Visualize the mind as a lake. When your thoughts are tranquil and calm, the surface of the lake is like glass. However, when a discordant or negative thought enters your mind, it creates a ripple on the surface of the mind-lake, and as these gather force, they become destructive waves.

Every time a disturbing thought of worry, fear, or any other negative emotion arises, push this through under the surface of the mind-lake and it will disappear.

The purpose of this spiritual exercise is to keep the surface of the mind-lake as calm as possible at all times.

I also value the spiritual mountaintop exercise. The spiritual mountaintop is the mind-consciousness that you will achieve when you climb from the shadow-filled valley of the mortal mind. When sickness, pain, worries, and fears of the mortal valleys of life become oppressive, you visualize yourself climbing a mountain. There, on the spiritual mountaintop, concentrate on the eternal reality and splendor of God, and your spiritual eyes may see beyond the veil of the earth's horizon to the immortal realm of the soul's future immortality.

My one aim is to seek to help you avoid going through the long, tedious hours of study which I went through, trying, failing, and then suddenly reaching a solution. I have a tremendous desire to help others to understand that intuition, or any psychic or occult phase, is not at all mystical. It is simply something which you study and practice, going over and over it, until the glorious day arrives when you feel that at last you have perfected the method.

As time goes on, you will find too that the more you use your intuitive power, the more accurate it becomes. This can be tested even in little things, such as telling the time of day. Instead of glancing at the clock when you wish to know the time, just depend on your intuition, saying, "I wonder what time it is," and immediately the voice of intuition will come through.

Sometimes you *feel,* rather than see, something. All of a sudden, you will seem to *feel* that it is seven o'clock, for instance, and I would wager if you were to look at the clock, it would be that time.

Do not become discouraged, though, if you make a few mistakes. I always tell others, "I am no different from you. Anything I can do, you also can do." However, I never give myself the credit for this. I have always depended on the Infinite to guide and to help me, especially where intuition is concerned.

Many have said to me, "I wish I had your faith." I feel extremely sorry for those people, because they are so bewildered and unhappy. All they would have to do would be to turn within themselves to find the true answer. That is why people who are psychic, or intuitive, cannot honestly take credit for anything accurate that they tell a person. I cannot stress too much that one should never become egotistical.

I know it is a boost to one's pride to have someone say, "Oh, you were so right; your intuition was perfect." But that is when you should immediately turn within yourself, realizing that it really was not you who gave this advice. It was intuition, dependent on the Infinite, that must be given credit for the answers.

When I receive praise, I feel as though the person is talking about someone else, not me.

Have you ever noticed how very strange silence is? There is a certain silence that comes just before a storm, almost as if everything is at a standstill. Death brings a strange silence, as if the lips of those you love, which are now closed in this world, will open thanksgiving in the next. In life, the whole of man works in silence: there is a silence connected with each part of your body, each one performing its particular function. The stars move silently in their various courses. A great idea inevitably takes form in the silence of the individual person. If we are really wise, the things that are most sacred to us we keep to ourselves in silence.

You will find, too, that your intuition is very still. There is no restlessness connected with it. As with anything pertaining to the occult, there is a calmness and a profound silence. I am against anything which is done in a manner that calls attention to what one is doing. To my way of thinking, trying to accomplish something in a quiet manner is far more effective than "shouting from the housetops."

Quite some time ago, I became very apprehensive over my husband. He had taken a short trip, and it seemed as if every time the phone rang I expected to hear some bad news. I did not learn how accurate this intuition was until the next morning, when upon his return, my husband mentioned that on the way home he had seen a person standing in the road, signaling for a lift. My husband said he had put on the brakes and had started to slow up when a strong feeling came over him not to pick that person up, that he would be sorry if he did.

Since my husband has always had a great deal of concern for the other person and because this person was a woman, he had begun to feel guilty because he had sped on and left her standing there at the roadside. But he also noticed that as he looked at the woman in the rear view mirror, she was standing in a very ungainly manner.

About a week later there was a story in all of the papers that this hitchhiker had murdered a motorist who had stopped at her signal. My husband shuddered to think what his fate might have been. It was disclosed that the "woman" had been a man in disguise, who thought that feminine garb would more easily stop a sympathetic motorist.

My husband said he would never forget the feeling that came over him as he approached that person. He had noticed instinctively that while "she" was quite a nice looking woman, she was heavily made up—no doubt to hide the masculine features. As he drew nearer the hitchhiker, he suddenly felt as if I were very close to him. He sensed that I was worried, and this sensation heightened his apprehension. He quickly reached over and locked the door, because he felt that, if he had stopped, that person would have forcibly entered the car.

Many times if I am worried or upset, my husband will sense my distress and will come home immediately. Once a young man came to my door and said that he had read my column for many years, and he insisted upon meeting me. Previously, I had told the young man through a letter that I am no longer able to grant personal interviews because my mail is so heavy. I told him that I appreciated his interest in my work and that I would help him all I could through the mail. Somehow I had felt that this person would not heed my words.

He chose a night when I was alone and my husband would be quite late (I did not expect Mr. Lauer until eleven or twelve P.M.) to make his uninvited visit. The moment my hand was on the doorknob, I sensed that there was trouble on the other side of that door. The young man pushed his foot in the door and forced his way in. I immediately recognized his name and told him that I knew who he was and that I was a little perturbed that he had not paid attention to my secretary's note to him telling him that I did not grant personal interviews.

He protested that he had hitchhiked nearly three thousand miles, and he insisted upon seeing me. I felt that I must immediately send out a thought to my husband which would bring him home at once.

The young man proclaimed that he had been sent to me in order that we might experience death together and thereby attain the highest pinnacle of consciousness. I felt it was best to keep him talking and to try to buy time until my husband arrived. I tuned in on the Divine Mind. Whenever I have the feeling that I hear the words "Be still and know that I am God," I know that I will come out of the situation all right.

My husband said later that he had been in a store buying some articles when suddenly he felt as if he had to put everything back and rush right home. When he arrived, he was not too surprised to see the situation that awaited him.

The young man was most belligerent toward Mr. Lauer. He asked my husband how long he had been married to me, and Mr. Lauer replied that we had been married a long, long time.

"Well, don't expect to have her that long again," the young man said. "Can't you leave the room, Mr. Lauer? I want to talk with your wife alone."

My husband replied, "I have no desire to leave. Evidently you aren't on the level of consciousness that I am."

"Well, don't you have any friends at all?"

"Yes, we have many friends," my husband told him, "but we choose our friends. We don't have them forced upon us."

My husband is a very mild-mannered person, but he did become quite upset and he told the man to leave immediately, or he would call the authorities.

Here again it was intuition that warned me and alerted my husband to the danger I was in.

Another very vivid example of intuition concerned my daughter. Tina had been very interested in a young man, and she planted two little trees in front of our home, which she laughingly named "Bud," after her boyfriend, and "Carol," after a very dear girlfriend of hers.

One day Tina noticed that "Bud" was beginning to lose its leaves. No matter what she did, the tree just would not respond.

When Tina asked me about it, I said little, but I definitely received a strong impression that the dying tree was a symbol that Bud would not live very long.

As the months went by, the little tree began to wither, and Tina felt upset by its poor health. The tree became so deteriorated that we had to destroy it.

Then one morning Bud called Tina to tell her that he was taking a trip up to the mountains with two friends. Although they had been dating steadily for some time, they had not announced an engagement. In fact, Tina remembered later, Bud had always refused to discuss the future in any way. Tina felt a powerful impression of danger that morning when Bud called, but because, technically, she was no more than a friend, she did not feel that she could assert her will upon him.

"Be careful," was all she could say. "Please do be careful."

That night my daughter got up and came into my bedroom. "Mother," she said softly. "I know that something has happened to Bud."

The next day we watched the news on television and learned that three young men had gone off a dangerous curve on a mountain road. One of the young men had been killed. It was Bud.

A few months later, after Bud's death, Tina came home from work pale and shaken. "My goodness, Tina," I said. "You look as if you had seen a ghost."

"I don't know if you would call Bud a ghost or not," she said, "but I know I saw him."

According to Tina, Bud had suddenly appeared in the road in front of her automobile. Tina had slammed on her brakes, startled, because the image of Bud had appeared almost in front of the cemetery in which he had been buried.

For a moment it seemed as if she had only had a terrible dream in which Bud had died. The reality was there in front of her automobile. Bud was alive, smiling at her, holding an index finger in the air and shaking it at her. The motion seemed to be one of playful scolding, and Tina received the impression that Bud was saying: "You just escaped something terrible. Next time, be more cautious!"

Then Tina noticed the ambulances and police cars howling past her halted auto. An awful collision had just occurred at the intersection. Three cars were involved. People lay sprawled on the street, one obviously in critical condition.

If Tina had not been stopped by the image of the now-vanished Bud, she would have been right in the midst of that dreadful accident.

Spiritualism does have its place in our lives. I do not believe in relying on spirit communication for tips on the stock market or weather forecasts. I do not believe that those who have passed on have many opportunities to relay such information; if they did they would not have time to progress to higher spiritual planes. However, I do feel that in times of stress, those who thought a great deal of us may be permitted to give us a warning from the "other side."

If you have learned to use your intuition properly, you will know how to recognize these warnings and you will never be frightened by such messages. I have been able to test such admonitions over a period of several years, and I have found that whenever I feel the presence of anyone dear to me who has passed on, it is most often a warning to be especially cautious on that day.

When you have mastered intuition, you will become a great help to those around you who may need your words of advice. They too will realize that your only desire is to help them. You must tell them without hesitation that the moment they begin to turn within, to know themselves, that they will be on the right road to attaining calmness and complete peace, which truly passes all understanding.

Soon you will have so many wonderful memories that they will more than compensate for the past sorrows which you have encountered. Complete harmony with even one other person can result in your looking upon grief, unhappiness, and distasteful incidents with much more tolerance than you could otherwise bear.

I have a thought within my mind that I must pass on to you: Never allow your imagination and your emotions to get the best of you.

Let us say that you are jealous of someone and you permit your emotions and your imagination to get out of hand. You could, in your mind's eye, picture all sorts of things, and thereby cause your own destruction. If you allow the two mischief-makers, imagination and emotion, to take control of your helm, you may end up on the rocky shore. You must always be the master of your emotions and you must learn to keep your imagination subdued.

You will find that a mild form of intuition may also pay off in your studies. If you are strongly interested in a subject, you will find that your intuition can guide you to the correct answers.

If you have, let us say, a stiff examination coming up, let your mind concentrate upon passages of your text for about three minutes. Then, in your mind's eye, go over those passages word for word, as you saw them in the text. After practice, you can read anything, fix it in your mind, and repeat it exactly as written.

I have studied music for many years, and I can memorize any piece of music that I desire by using this method, note by note, without any slip-ups.

"I never see you use any sheet music," people often say to me.

Those folks with no musical training may feel that I play by ear, but a trained musician, who has played the same piece which I am performing, knows very well if I were to miss even a single note or if I were not to play the piece exactly as it was written.

This book has been promising you that you can get what you want out of life, and you are learning how you can do just that, regardless of what your goals may be.

Chapter Six

How to Cross Out
Your Psychic Bondage

*There is no need to live with fear and apprehension in your life.
In this chapter you will find a new method for releasing the psychic bonds which prevent your life from being more enjoyable
and rewarding.*

ARE YOU AWARE of the fact that you may actually be
bound by the very thoughts and words which you use
every day? When I tell you to cross out your bondage,
I am referring to any habit, any unkind thought, or any negative
concept that you may have.

As you know, the cross has been used throughout the ages
as a symbol of inspiration to many. It is possible for everyone
to use a mental cross to erase the words and thoughts which bind
them. There can be no evil in your life unless you give the negative forces power by your thoughts and deeds. Strive now to
cross out hate, resentment, criticism, and the limiting thoughts
that are holding you back.

Let us say that you would like to go into a new business venture, yet you do not want to release the old files and books which you have kept on your former business. It would be almost impossible to succeed in a new enterprise as long as you do not let go of the old ideas and the old conditions which dominated your former establishment. In your mind's eye, you must cross out the old business and make way for the new venture.

If you had a business where tools were required, you must get rid of all these old implements. If you cherish these objects from your former business, you are subconsciously holding onto your old work because you are not quite certain whether you will be successful in your new venture. Only when you put those old tools out of sight or sell them will you have enthusiasm for the enterprise that you are about to undertake.

As another example, let us suppose that you had owned a knitting shop and you had kept all the leftover yarn. The new business which you would like to enter is that of owning a beauty shop. If you allow negative thoughts to draw you back to the old shop where you continue to sort through the remaining yarn, you are subconsciously saying, "Well, I can always go back into the knitting business if I don't succeed with my beauty shop." Such mental behavior would be blocking all the wonderful channels that might be open to you if you were to pack away the old yarn and plunge full force into the beauty shop venture.

You must get rid of the old in order to make way for the new. If I repeat myself, I do this purposely so that your subconscious mind will pick up this important thought.

In your mind's eye, you should visualize the word and idea of "knitting shop." Then you should mentally cross out and erase "knitting shop" and write in "beauty shop." If you do this properly, it will be almost impossible *not* to have your new business prosper, because you have crossed out the limitation from your mind.

I am including this chapter in my book because so many clients have written to me over the years and told me that they have used affirmations or meditation, but they have not obtained any results. What, they all ask, is wrong? They always provide me with an answer when, further along in their letters, they inadvertently reveal that they are holding onto an old thought or idea while they have the affirmation in mind or when they are deep in meditation. Such a holding action prevents the very thing they most desire from occurring. One must be free of the old and receptive to the new when he uses affirmations.

A wife once wrote to me because she wanted her husband to stop drinking. She told me that she had been using the affirmation, "As you think of drinking, you will no longer have the desire to do so."

But in her mind, she had been visualizing her husband with drink in hand. No wonder he would not stop! Can you see what I am trying to put across? I am certain that you can. While this woman was affirming those beautiful thoughts, her own subconscious was holding onto the image of the old habit. If she had only known about this cross-out formula, I believe that she would have been spared many years of distressing conditions.

In your mind's eye you can readily picture a white cross going through the hatred, the resentment, and the condemnation which you may hold for yourself or for others. This very moment, stop and think of someone for whom you harbor resentment. Visualize a white cross being stamped on that very idea or past action which has made you feel upset. If you are sincere, you will have to admit that you suddenly felt much more light-hearted after you erased the old hurt or the long-nurtured hatred.

In our imagination, let us take a stroll through a park. We spy a group of senior citizens, made up primarily of men, seated leisurely on some park benches. They are waving their hands and talking mournfully to each other about what a sorry state of affairs the world is in.

"Why don't we have the good old days back?" one silver-haired fellow moans. Another complains of being constantly ill. Yet another whines because his pension is not sufficient and he is always poor. After a time they leave each other and shuffle off to their homes or apartments, each one feeling more miserable than he did before their impromptu discussion group.

If the elderly would only get together and talk about the pleasant things that have occurred in their lives, their words might inspire one of their more dour fellows to at last begin a search for the good. Old folks should be reminiscing about the wonderful things that have happened to them with the realization that through growing older they have gained wisdom.

To make matters worse, so many elderly people harbor an unforgiving attitude toward someone, and this in turn affects their own health. Here again, they have been so busy cherishing the old and the negative that they have not made provision for new thoughts, new inspirations, and new opportunities.

I hope that by the time you finish reading this chapter you will, by your own admission of negative thoughts, erase them or cross them out entirely. Such an erasure can mean the difference between success or failure in achieving your goals, the difference between happiness and unhappiness in your personal relationships, and the difference between being healthy or unhealthy in your mind and body. By crossing out the negative, you make room for the new thoughts which you should be holding.

Let us say that right now you begin to think of someone who has hurt you in the past. Immediately you bristle within yourself and your mind begins to dwell upon that old injury. Visualize exactly what that person did to harm you; then erase the image with the white cross.

This is not a Pollyannish way of living; this is not wishful thinking. This is the wonderful act of erasing a negative limitation from one's mind, just as one would wipe clean a slate.

As you use the crossing-out formula, you will feel very relieved, and the very act of erasing the hurt serves as a kind of blessing to the person who has hurt you. I realize that you must try this formula before you will believe that it really works, but I can guarantee that it does.

You will recall that I mentioned in an earlier chapter my contention that anyone who has had cancer has at some time nurtured resentment, anger, or hatred toward another person.

Had these people gone to the person who was the object of their hatred or had they erased the memory of the resentment with the white cross, they might have made their situation an entirely different one. In time to come, I firmly believe that medical doctors will ask people to rid themselves of their fears, their hatreds, and their resentments before effective healing can take place.

I know that many of you who read this, especially if you happen to be a victim of cancer, may become very angry with me and say that accusations are ridiculous. You may tell me that you are not angry with anybody. Perhaps, you may admit, you had a terrible feud with someone twenty years ago, but you certainly are not quarreling with anyone now.

But you see it does not make any difference how long ago it was that you were filled with hatred. I know that some of you are ready to ask me, "Do you mean that if I had never had such thoughts, I may not have been a victim of cancer?"

I am convinced that I can truthfully answer "yes" to that questions because if you are as honest with me as I am with you, you will go back in your mind and find what it was that caused you to feel that hatred or resentment.

A young woman who had cancer told me that she had resented very much the fact that her mother, several years before, had given her a few dollars, put her on a bus, and told her to make her own way in life. Being pushed out into the world in such a manner had been such a shock to her that she had harbored ill feelings toward her mother until the very day in which she confided in me.

Even though the young woman had not yet been to a doctor, I warned her at once that such long-nurtured feelings of hatred could be breeding cancer within her body. I knew her well enough to be very blunt with her and I suggested that she visit her doctor at once. She followed my advice, and her doctor did indeed diagnose cancer. Fortunately, the surgeons were able to operate in time and the woman is perfectly well today.

We are on this planet for such a short length of time. Time is too precious to waste holding resentful or hateful thoughts against anyone. Each person is held accountable for his thoughts, words, and deeds. One must not allow himself to become mired in the swill of prejudice, the cesspool of hatred, and the dismal swamp of resentment.

Remember at all times to use your mental blackboard. Picture yourself back in school with a teacher who writes one lesson upon the board, then erases it to present yet another valuable set of rules for your educational benefit. If all of us could only learn to cross out our resentments when we were children, we would not carry our hurts and hatreds around with us through life. Complete happiness and contentment and better and brighter lives are the reward of those who do not hesitate to apply this formula and immediately cross out their fears, frustrations, and feuds.

I knew one gentleman who felt that he was not understood by his wife and children. In a kind of self-defense, he would become so engrossed in his television programs that he would not hear what was being said to him by any member of his family. He had subconsciously plugged his ears. A visitor to the home, however, could speak to him in a normal tone of voice, and he would respond at once.

There are so many wives who complain that they can talk and talk to their husbands, but the men do not seem to hear a word that they say. If one is able to gain insight into the husbands' psyches, one would see that they regard their wives' chatter as a non-stop, long-playing record that repeats the same tired, nagging chant. There are a great many husbands who subconsciously afflict themselves with deafness.

If only these couples would realize that all they have to do is to erase, to cross out all their negative thoughts. If they were to use such an affirmation as, "There is harmony between us and I rise above negative behavior, and therefore, petty irritations do not annoy me," I would wager that they would develop a new appreciation of each other and learn to live together in a harmonious relationship. Never hesitate a moment to erase the word "incompatibility" with the white cross.

If you are complaining that you have no money, immediately cross out the word "no" and leave the word "money." Once you have done this, you will be amazed at the paths which will be revealed to you. If you have a family, be certain to affirm, "Our financial condition cannot be limited." There is no place for the selfish "my" if you are part of a family unit.

As I have told you, everything which I relay to you in this book has been developed and practiced by me and my clients over a period of many years. This is why I was so eager to write this book. I knew that once you were able to grasp these formulas, the benefits would never leave you, and you in turn might become an instrument of succor to some other person.

Years ago, when I would sit in my office dictating psychometric analyses for my clients, I would wonder if there were not some formula which everyone might use to free themselves from psychic bondage. Then one day the image of the white cross came into my mind, and I saw it blot out the very troubles which had been bothering me. I was thrilled when the inspiration came to me, and I am thrilled now to be able to share it with you.

You may be somewhat skeptical of this method of crossing out your bondage when you first begin to experiment with it, but I know that the day will come when you will discover that the psychic formula did work for you. The method is so simple that once it has become a part of your life you will wonder how on earth you ever got along without it.

If you dwell on a high state of consciousness and your unity is with God, you cannot help agreeing with the psalmist who reveals in the ninety-first psalm that "He that dwelleth in the secret place of the Most High shall abide under the shadow of the Almighty."

You have come to realize, along with Job, that "The thing which I fear cometh to me." You should never be fearful or apprehensive of what lies ahead of you.

The ancient Hebrew word for evil is *aven*, which means "nothing." You can block evil directly out of your life by refusing to talk about it, by refusing to become upset by it, and by always keeping in mind that it is nothing.

I know that some of you are thinking that such a method is easier said than done, but if you would try this formula for a period of two weeks, I know that you will be able to report many new changes in your life.

I would indeed be very naive if I were to claim that there were no evil people in the world. To recognize their existence, however, does not mean that we must associate with them if we do not care to. If you know someone of bad influence who is involving himself in a loved one's life, you can work a mighty change on that person by blotting out the word "evil" and replacing it with a blessing of good for that individual.

As you learn to cross out negative thoughts from your mind, you will begin to feel as if there is a oneness, a togetherness with the Divine Mind that you have never felt before. But it is up to you to erase those thoughts of negativism almost as rapidly as they might occur.

I am able to enter a public building or attend a social gathering and tell at once which of the people sitting there are resentful, upset, or guilty of harboring thoughts of hatred. I am also able to determine which people are practicing the method of white-cross erasure or any technique which is similar to it in purpose.

Once one begins to employ such a positive formula, he has tapped the workings of an immutable law. If the various denominations of the orthodox churches were to emphasize such methods as the white cross for freeing their people from psychic bondage, I am certain that these formulas would bring about a unity of the many sects and church bodies which is so terribly lacking at the present time. Nothing would aid the cause of ecumenism more than a universal conclusion that each person contained within himself a part of Divine Intelligence.

A Chinese proverb aptly states: "The longest journey starts with a single step."

An unknown author observed: "What we are to be, we are now becoming."

George McDonald noted that, "A man is in bondage to whatever he cannot part with."

How anxious I have been to write this chapter so that every reader of this book may put into use the formula that will help him to cross out all of his negative habits. Robert Louis Stevenson wrote, "Everything sooner or later sits down to a banquet of consequences." Now that you have begun using the cross-out formula, you will find that your banquet of consequences may actually be one to which you will look forward to with eager anticipation.

Chapter Seven

Mastering Creative Concentration

As you read this chapter title, I can picture you with a furrowed brow. Concentration, you are thinking, is a difficult art. I think that you are in for a surprise. When you learn the technique given in this chapter, your furrowed brow will become smooth and tranquil.

THE WORD "CONCENTRATION" conjures up an image of someone trying very hard to keep a certain object, person, or idea in his mind. People who concentrate in such a manner are doing the very thing which they should avoid.

May I suggest that you sit in a very comfortable chair and relax. I do not mean that you should go into a trance, nor do I mean that you should become so visibly limp that you look like a rag doll. Simply sit comfortably and do not think of any one particular subject. For about five minutes, just *relax.*

After five minutes of complete relaxation, I suggest that you concentrate on one problem in particular that is bothering you.

If you have been concerned because you have not heard from a certain person, concentrate on that individual and see what impression comes into your mind. If you receive a feeling of nonchalance or indifference, you may have received an indication that the person is either busy or has no desire to get in touch with you at the present time.

If you wish, you may visualize this person and at the same time form a question in your mind, such as, "Why haven't you written or phoned me?" An impression will then come back to you via mental telepathy, as we have discussed previously.

If you need a visible object as a means of aiding concentration, you may obtain an ordinary glass of drinking water and set it before you. Others favor a sheet of plain white paper. I have become so accustomed to concentrating that I do not even have to close my eyes any more. I can concentrate with my eyes wide open and with no one the wiser. If you should require such aids as water or paper, do not expect to see anything in the glass or on the sheet, as that would be "crystal gazing." We will take up that subject a bit later, but in this chapter we are discussing concentration.

If you are concentrating correctly, it will be almost as if you have drawn a straight line from your mind directly to whatever object on which your attention is focused. After practice, all other thoughts will seem to be automatically erased from your mind.

To repeat a word of caution, you must never concentrate upon a person with the idea in mind of doing him any harm. The law of compensation will rule in the end and that which you wish for another will come back to you.

I have had some people tell me that it takes a great deal out of them to concentrate. Strangely enough, it has exactly the opposite effect on me. I feel at ease and completely relaxed after concentration, as if it has been a wonderful, calming adventure.

After concentrating for a certain amount of time, you may say, "My mind just jumps all over. I think of everything I have ever gone through. I think of many things that I thought I had forgotten." I would say that this is the first step in getting your mind trained to enter certain channels of concentration.

After this primary upheaval of your mind, you will gradually get to the point where there will be few thoughts in your mind other than the ones on which you wish to concentrate.

I would suggest that you begin your regimen of concentration with periods of five minutes a day for the first week. The following week, try ten minutes. A week later try fifteen minutes. How long you wish to concentrate is entirely up to you, but I would suggest that, at least near the beginning of your experimentation, you do not attempt to retain mental anchorage for one-hour or two-hour periods. Such sessions would be entirely too much for you, and you would produce no more results than if you were to start out gradually.

When you begin regular concentration periods, you may find yourself thinking of a particular person. You may suddenly have the feeling that the person is wishing you would contact him. Such a sensation is usually an indication that someone is thinking of getting in touch with you. Should this activity occur during a concentration session, I would suggest that you write down the impression as a reminder if that person should contact you within a few days.

Concentration may also be wonderful if a person does not feel too well. A brief period of concentration will result in his nerves becoming very relaxed, and the session definitely will not take anything from him. The only reason that some people claim that they feel tired and nervous after intense concentration is that they are going about it incorrectly. If you put a tremendous amount of effort into an improper kind of concentration, you can easily bring on a headache.

Many years ago, I realized that the less effort I put into concentration, the more effective it was. All that is necessary is simply to sit quietly and relax, using the glass of water or sheet of white paper if you like.

Sometimes people ask me if one can use concentration in order to achieve more restful sleep. I can assure all you insomniacs that you can, but once again, you must engage in concentration with as little effort as possible. Do not force your mind into deep, hard thinking, saying over and over to yourself, "I'm going to sleep! I'm going to sleep!"

When you retire at night, you should never count sheep or that sort of thing. Instead, picture a very beautiful forest, a lovely pastoral scene, a peaceful mountain meadow, or any place that you would particularly like to be. Soon you will relax and fall sound asleep.

This is a form of concentration that is passive, and I have always maintained that a passive form of concentration is more effective than one jammed with effort. If you put a great deal of stress on your concentration, by the time you have achieved a mastery of the technique you will be too exhausted to appreciate the results.

At this point I feel that I should give you a word of warning: *You must not use your imagination!*

It is easy to sit and imagine all sorts of things, but there is a vast difference between concentration and imagination. In true concentration, your mind becomes very much like a silver sheet within your mind, a silver sheet which is very beautiful and very illuminating. However, very little will appear upon the silver sheet unless you are concentrating on either a person or an object.

Suppose you, like so many people who write to me, are convinced that someone you like very much is equally as fond of you. If you concentrate on this person and receive a feeling of indifference or a sensation of coolness, then you may rest assured that you have only imagined that this person likes you.

As this point you should take hold of yourself and tell yourself that you are now going to face facts and not pretend that someone likes you when you have received such a cold, indifferent feeling from them during concentration. Properly executed, concentration should be able to give you a balance where your emotions are concerned.

Often people interpret a slight word or gesture as an indication of great devotion or admiration on the part of an individual who may only have been indulging in a simple act of friendliness or kindness without intending anything of a serious nature.

Many times when someone has told me that so-and-so is very fond of her because he smiled at her, I frankly tell her that she is interpreting his actions according to the way in which she wants that person to feel about her. If someone really does think a great deal of you, you should receive a very warm feeling as you concentrate on him.

As in all teachings, belief is the one secret; but it has to be belief without doubt, for even as the soul finds itself believing in the Infinite, to that soul the Infinite is very personal. All mystics have stated that they have talked to God. They believe this very firmly, and they feel that the experience has been so very personal that all doubt has been swept away. Thus it is in all phases of teaching. Even in concentration, belief is the most important factor.

You cannot enter into concentration by saying rather dubiously to yourself, "Oh, I know this won't work." If you harbor a negative attitude, you will find that nothing will work for you.

Remember, though, that as you apply these truths, you must be prepared for many changes which will come into your life. To utilize these psychic formulas and have conditions continue as they were would be impossible. A change will definitely take place; and when you master the art of creative concentration, you will discover, as I have, that much can be learned simply by letting yourself be led.

Andrew Carnegie once said, "The man who acquires the ability to take full possession of his own mind may take possession of everything else to which he is justly entitled."

Underline the word "justly." Concentration will enable to you to determine that which can, and should, be justly yours. If you should hurt another to achieve your goals, you will only bring great hurt upon yourself.

I have always expected that which I have wanted to be in my life, yet I have always been careful to ask first, "Will my obtaining this object of my desire hurt anyone else?"

My answer has always had to be "no" before I could continue my affirmations, visualizations, and concentration.

"Will this personal success cause someone to go without so that I may gain?"

Again, the answer has had to be "no." I have learned to discipline my mind to achieve that which I expect, and a disciplined mind cannot be led by others. That is why I am so positive in my analyses and in my writings. I know within myself if the written word that I am conveying is what I want communicated to you.

Such knowing is within your soul as it is mine, but the secret is that you must know that your actions are correct and that you are not being guided by your imagination. When you have learned to concentrate as I have, you will not imagine. You will concentrate easily and comfortably, and you will not be misled by imagination.

I have heard so many people in my kind of work complain that they become so tired, so worn out. But they become exhausted while engaged in psychic activities only because they allow fatigue to take over. If one is properly attuned to Divine Intelligence, there is no weariness, but only a feeling of elation because concentration is effortless. If you have to force concentration, it will not bring the desired results at all.

In a sense, concentration also becomes meditation. The emotions will be stilled if concentration is rightly practiced, and once this has taken place meditation becomes quite easily achieved.

Unfortunately, there are those who would misuse this great gift. As much as I try to warn people against psychic abuses, certain individuals insist upon concentration upon those things which will bring harm to others. *Use wisdom in concentrating.*

My files contain the case histories of men and women who have concentrated on achieving terrible things, even death for their mates so that they might be free to marry their lovers. In many cases, it has been the girlfriend or the boyfriend who has passed on.

Then, in puzzled remorse, they come to me with the question, *"Why?"*

These tragic individuals had no right to wish harm to other people. Had they wished their spouses well, concentrated on bringing them happiness and contentment, perhaps things might have worked out more to their satisfaction.

Concentration is powerful, but so are the laws of retribution!

Before you begin to practice concentration or any of these psychic formulas, take some time to examine your motives. Be completely honest with yourself and carefully examine the reasons why you wish to attain certain goals. You may rest assured that I am cautious about what I concentrate upon, because I *know* that the results will be at my door.

Chapter Eight

How to Develop Your Psychic Abilities

In this chapter I will show you how you may be able to discover whether or not you have any psychic talents, and if so, how to develop them. You will find that there are many ways in which a hidden ESP ability may express itself, and there are many ways in which it may be developed.

Distance makes absolutely no difference to ESP abilities. The person whom you wish to contact may be seated next to you or he may be 4,000 miles away; it is all the same to the hidden power of your mind. But you must practice the exercises that I give you, and by all means keep at them. Do not just read these chapters and be done with them. I would much prefer you to take just one chapter at a time, reading it and studying it thoroughly, than to take them all, reading them casually, skipping over important aids in an effort to finish the book in a hurry.

Often a customer will leave a particular store and say to his spouse, "I don't know why I bought this article. I really didn't need it."

The store's salesman has in some way developed a psychic dominance that he may exercise upon a customer's will. Most salesman have taken a long time to develop this ability; although the mechanics of what they do may be almost completely sub-conscious and nameless to them, the good salesman realizes that to be successful in selling, a good deal depends upon his personality and his basic attitudes.

I realize, of course, that every reader of this book is not inter-ested in becoming a salesman. I simply use this illustration to point out that one does not have to go into trances in order to exercise psychic abilities. Salesmen are very active people, but most of them have developed enough psychic talent to be able to project their thoughts upon the mind of the customer to whom they are selling.

The more vigorous you are, the more dynamic force can be placed behind your psychic powers. If one is ill, convalescing, or weary, his ability to control psychic powers dissipates appre-ciably. Such conditions are definitely not propitious times for one to try to develop psychic talents. Both mental and physical strength should be restored and one should feel totally revived before he begins to practice psychic development.

Many teachers will advise you to meditate in order to develop your ESP abilities. Meditation is prayer, or being silent.

Meditation is fine, but I recommend that you do not overindulge in these periods of withdrawal.

The psychic power is a silent one, but to retreat into lengthy sessions of meditation in order to develop ESP talents may earn you a reputation for being odd. Do try to avoid this, because reputation for eccentricity too often blights the lives of those who try too hard to become well-known psychics. Use your common sense, and you will be a happier person, I assure you.

When I was very young, I became aware of the fact that I was psychic, but my mother refused to allow me to become obsessed with the paranormal. Often she would say to me, "I want you to be a normal little girl. If we have company and something comes to you that you feel you must tell someone, that is all right; but for heaven's sake, don't become odd!"

When one deliberately seeks to develop his psychic prowess, he should not enter into his studies too rigorously at first. Practice your exercises for fifteen to twenty minutes, or even an hour if you feel you are able to, and then go on leading a perfectly normal existence. You will get much more out of your studies, as well as your life, if you do not gain a reputation for eccentricity.

It seems to be a truism that you will rarely find a pessimist who is a psychic. One must be optimistic to develop the true extent of his paranormal abilities. Even though the optimist cannot say that there is no evil, he does not dwell upon the negative aspects of life.

When a psychic talent is developed, it soon presents an awareness of itself. You will find that you must multiply your gifts and talents, and by usage, you will increase what you now possess. You must learn to subdue and to control emotions and temper, as well as negative thinking and actions. And, of course, it goes without saying that one must never resent or hate anyone.

It is absolutely impossible for one to develop any psychic power if there is hatred in the heart: it just will not work.

In every chapter I have written, I have stressed the fact that hate poisons one's mind and body, often causing one to attract sickness, accidents, and disasters. By actually blessing an enemy and releasing him to God, we are living under the law of love. One does not have to love everyone personally, but spiritually he must have a feeling of compassion for everyone.

You can definitely develop psychic power. It may surprise you when I say that everyone is actually as psychic as I am; the only difference is that I have developed this power.

When you meet someone, note your first impression. If your psychic power is there at all, the impression you have formed will be correct.

Many times I have heard people say, "I just didn't like that person the first time I met him, but I thought I could be wrong." I doubt, though, that you would be wrong if you are psychically attuned. Perhaps the person needs someone other than you in his sphere, and that is why you received those feelings. Now, that does not mean that you should dislike the person. It does mean, however, that you should not force a friendship with him. You must learn to use diplomacy, and you must not become sensitive if a person does not agree with you in your thinking.

I have had people ask, "Why do you not use this psychic power to get rich, to know horse race winners, and so on?"

ESP is not to be used in this manner, because one would then begin to live by games of chance, rather than by earning his livelihood, and this would be perverting a power that is intended to help someone with a problem, rather than to make easy money. Is it not better to help a troubled soul in distress than to tell him who will win a horse race? I have gone to Las Vegas on several occasions and I have experimented with gambling. I can say that certain methods may be used, but there is no fun in gambling if you can win all the time. You may say that is an odd opinion, but is it? I can concentrate, let us say, upon three bars coming up—oh yes, they will come up—but I feel as if I helped the machine by concentrating. While I am not really hurting anyone by winning, I am using ESP in the wrong manner, and therefore I will not do it. I would much rather put a person's mind at ease concerning his future than to have him hold scads of money in his hands that would be lost anyway by repeated gambling forays. The gambler is never quite satisfied.

Being psychic is interesting, and many times it enables you to know if a person is using your friendship to pick your brains, so to speak. I find that people who are genuinely gifted usually are sincere people. There are those who are not honest, but they do not last long and become obscure very quickly.

When I made two television appearances with Pamela Mason, wife of actor James Mason and a very opinionated lady, friends asked me if I was not afraid to meet her. I could not see why I should be afraid to meet anyone, because I am sincere in what I do. Pamela Mason is known to be outspoken, but so am I. She was very nice to me, and she seemed very pleased with the analysis that I did on the air for her. I had no preparation, as she does not meet her guests ahead of time. When you go on the set, you are on the air; I like this about her program, as well as Joe Pyne's, a television host known for his brusque, confrontational manner. There is no behind-the-scenes talking. It is all spontaneous.

I have had offers to give information for people who wished to collect rewards. I would never take rewards of any kind. I feel here too that if I can help, fine. But I do not feel that I should give advice unless asked for it, and I confine this to analysis. I do not think the police want anyone trying to do their work. They are capable. If any officials wish my help, I am here. But I will not push myself on to anyone. I also feel that if you use psychic ability merely to brag about those for whom you do analyses, you are wrong. Name dropping is in poor taste. My list of celebrated clients is long, but their names are strictly confidential with me.

It is not important whether a person agrees with you or not. The important thing is to learn to develop your psychic power to the point that you, yourself, are satisfied with it.

In my opinion, a very good exercise for you to do is to sit quietly in a chair, close your eyes, and picture a screen in front of you as big and as wide as a movie screen. At the same time think of a particular problem or person. It will be almost as if a picture is projected upon this screen from your mind, and you will be surprised at some of the things that flash on this screen.

Later on, you may dispense with the visualization of a screen and easily receive impressions or feelings. If you want the psychic power in the form of "seeing," that is the way you will receive it. If you want it in the form of automatic writing, that is the way it will come to you. Some want paranormal talent in the form of materialization, and they become very good materialization mediums. I, however, have always desired the gift to take form as impressions or feelings, and they have proven to be very accurate for me.

When you try the screen method, do not try to see what you want to see. There is a catch here that many people do not want to get into. You can want to see almost anything, but when you get the right impression on your mental screen, you do not have to force anything.

If you were to say to yourself, "I wonder if Mary likes me," and then think, "Of course she does, of course she does," you have not received a psychic impression. You should remain very quiet, and if Mary really does like you, you will get a feeling of contentment, as well as a feeling of affection. If, however, she actually does not like you, you will experience a feeling of antagonism.

Personally, I feel too much mystery has been made of the occult. If everyone would simply sit down and meditate, using the screen method, they could be just as psychic as the publicized seers.

There are people who are afraid of anything psychic. However, they shouldn't be, as there certainly is nothing eerie about it.

There are times when I am in the company of friends who are not aware of my psychic abilities and, therefore, are not hesitant when discussing ESP to tear the subject to pieces. When this occurs, I try to convince them how wrong they are. It seems to me that logic and common sense should be used in addition to one's psychic gifts. There is the danger of becoming obsessed. Many who are engaged in psychic work have become so obsessed with their abilities that they can think of nothing else twenty-four hours a day. To me, this would be very dull indeed.

Once again, I suggest that you try very hard to visualize this screen of which I spoke, thinking perhaps of someone who is ill. Do not think, "I wonder if they are going to get better." Just place the person in your mind and you will know.

I do not approve of tests where cards are used as a means of testing ESP accuracy. It just does not seem important to me whether I read the nine of spades or the nine of diamonds twenty times in a row. I truly do not think this is a real test of one's paranormal talents.

If you develop your psychic ability enough so that you may help other people as well as yourself, I think that is much more important than being able to call the ten of diamonds nine times out of ten when it is in a pack of fifty-two cards. Instead of devoting your time to ESP tests, visualize your mental screen; think of a problem or person and write down your impressions. These can be filed away and tested later on. If you do not let your imagination take over, you can become very proficient. I want you to be as accurate as possible, and the only way you achieve accuracy is by practice.

When you are mediating or trying to get a psychic impression, try to relax completely. There will be many new ideas coming into your mind once you enter into the psychic realm.

You may ask, "How will I know if it is imagination or real psychic ability?" Again, here is a test: Imagine how you would feel if a telegram arrived informing you that someone dear to you had passed on. Your grief and unhappiness would seem to be almost unbearable to you. Supposing, though, that you were to receive a second message saying that the first message had been sent in error! Your joy would be positively overwhelming, wouldn't it? Certainly you can imagine how you would feel if this were to happen to you. Through such an error, you would feel the terrible pangs of grief, yet these would be removed immediately by the exposure of the truth. Now, had true psychic ability been in command at the time the first message was received, you would have known that the message was incorrect. You would feel that grief was unnecessary. Can you see what I am trying to convey to you?

When psychic development is true and real, you can tell something is amiss. I can do this often while conversing with a client who wishes to convey a message to me without actually putting it into words. People might just as well come right out and say what is on their minds, as their hidden thoughts are clear to me.

Another facet of psychic development can be tested this way: Take an ordinary needle, thread it, and make a double strand of thread four or five inches long. Hold this double end of thread between your thumb and second finger, permitting the needle to hang freely over a sheet of paper on which you have drawn a circle. If the question you wish to ask can be answered "yes" or "no," then write "yes" at the top and bottom of the circle, and "no" at the two sides. If you want a more complete answer, write the alphabet around the circle, starting with "A" at the top and going clockwise. Then, holding the needle suspended over the paper, ask the question. The needle should swing back and forth, indicating "yes" or "no" or spelling out the correct answer. There have been tests on this use of psychic ability. I would venture to say that it could be classed in the same category with a ouija board, which, in some cases, is very accurate.

There are times, however, when a ouija board is most inaccurate. On occasion ouija boards seem to relay wrong messages in order to mislead a person. I mention this merely to show that unless the person practicing the occult phases is very sincere, there is no truth learned.

One must test repeatedly, however, before he can say with assurance that his psychic ability is real and genuine. Many times imagination will play a part, as well as superstition.

As an example, let's take an uncivilized native who knows absolutely nothing about electricity. We shall tell him to flip a switch and there will be a light. He looks utterly amazed; to him, this is magic. Until the fundamentals of electricity are explained to him, he is afraid of it. That is exactly the same thing superstition does to people. With fear, there can be no understanding.

When the native mentioned above is shown why the light goes on, he is no longer fearful. This is true also of a person who is afraid of the dark: until he can come to the mental conclusion that there is no reason for fear, he will remain fearful.

With psychic development, fear must be controlled and knowledge of the occult gained. When one understands the law of numbers, then the correct answers to problems are revealed. We can add and add, then add again, yet we always find that two and two are four. This is the same with psychic ability. If the answer is a true one, it does not change.

Study test, and be sure! Darkness will always battle light. Which will conquer? Light, of course! It is the same with superstition; once it is overcome, there is no longer any fear.

Another area of concentration is hypnosis. I urge you to be very cautious with hypnosis. I hasten to add, though, that there are many fine hypnotists who are specialists in their field. But to have just anyone take up hypnotism and practice it indiscriminately is of no value to psychic development.

I suggest, also, that you not dwell too much on your progress. By doing so, you become too self-centered, too engrossed. I cannot emphasize too strongly how wrong this is. If you develop a psychic ability, you will be aware of it.

The following is a valuable exercise practiced in the East.

One enters a state known as *samyama* by breathing deeply and slowly, at the same time meditating on the spiritual quality which he is endeavoring to attain. This consists of searching the inner self for true spiritual power. As God flows through His universe, He exists within as much as without.

As you breathe slowly, affirm:

"I now enter the sacred inner silence where transcendental intelligence exists; my inner eye is now opening with spiritual vision to see that which I am to do. My spiritual ear is now opening and I hear the intuitive voice of God which will guide me to my right destiny."

Now, sit in silence for a while and you will receive the guidance for which you ask.

I cannot emphasize too strongly that as long as you attune yourself to God, you will be successful. To do otherwise would only result in heartache and misgivings.

It is true that I have encountered criticism for making the above statement. However, I will always remember the wonderful person who helped me to achieve my psychic ability by saying, "Remember, Dorothy, so long as you give God the right to guide you in all spiritual things, ignoring all other forces, you will have correct and accurate psychic ability. The moment you let something or someone else take over, you are lost."

Instead of viewing money as the all-important thing, try to see the spiritual equivalent of that which you wish to attain. In other words, if you are in need of money, see it as a symbol of the thing you want; then the law will work for you. That thing will be formed in the matrix of the invisible universe and it will manifest itself under the natural law. And it will work, believe me! One can never set a financial value on health, happiness, true friends, love, or on dear ones. There is a spiritual equivalent that is much higher than the matter of money.

So long as you visualize money as being the means of health, wealth, or happiness, then its value is lost. Once you are able to look upon money as being merely a symbol, it will actually flow to you.

The Bible teaches, "Thou shalt have no other gods before me," and until we realize this, we will be miserable.

I hope that you who study this book will know with a knowledge that cannot be swayed that as soon as you become egotistical, or regard your own power as the source of your happiness, it will vanish!

When you donate to any charitable organization, by all means, do not give grudgingly. Bless the money and really mean it. Truly, it will return to you threefold, whether you want it to or not. Once again, the immutable law is at work.

The Upanishads say of a soul that has spiritual awareness, "He who has found the self, the world is his; indeed, he is the world itself."

As you develop the inner, spiritual psychic-self, you will hear an inner knowing, saying, "Be still, and know that I am God."

When this impression comes to me, I know then that either the right answer is very close or I have already received it.

Do not change your opinion once it is given.

Remember, you must practice humility, as the perfect sage is one who keeps his mind unified and humble.

Think of others in order to help build your spiritual strength, and send good thoughts out to those who may not even know you. These thoughts will reach the ones who need the most help. This is something that only you can give to others.

The less you think of your power, the more spiritually powerful you will become. Once you begin thinking of yourself only and become conceited, the power will be taken from you.

Perhaps you have heard of the friend who came to visit the great sculptor Michelangelo. The friend said, "Two weeks ago I came to see you and you were polishing that same piece of marble. Why do you labor so long over this?"

Michelangelo replied, "Trifles make perfection, but perfection is no trifle."

You must practice your spiritual exercises over and over until you can truthfully say, "I am sincerely trying to be perfect."

When someone compliments me on the psychic ability I possess, I feel rather strange, as I know that I am merely attuned to receive the right impression and therefore am not entitled to any personal praise.

A priceless gift is yours, believe me, if you are successful in developing psychic power. If you have but eyes to see, and ears to hear, it is as if an angel slumbers in your soul.

Refuse to let the demons of everyday living destroy you, my friends. Once again, I urge you to live a normal life. Do not become so engrossed within yourself that others will want to run from you.

Someone whom you may meet quite accidentally may be the very one who sees in you the one trait that can assist him in achieving even a small amount of success. Your psychic ability has been awakened! Use it correctly, and above all, be humble and grateful.

You too will be able to lead others, and even if only *one* is guided correctly, you will indeed have been well compensated.

So, watch—and see!

Chapter Nine

Helping Yourself to Happiness Through Psychometry

Psychometry is an art that may have been recognized more in the past than today. It is my hope that the ancient art of object reading will be used a great deal more in the future. The first requirement of a psychometrist is that he be completely honest with himself and with the clients he elects to serve. Psychometry may present the correct impression which might prevent someone from making a great error in his life. Psychometry may stop someone from making an improper investment or form signing an unwise business agreement. This ancient art may provide both the psychic and his client with an invaluable aid to living in our increasingly complex society.

W HEN I WAS VERY YOUNG, I discovered that I could tell a great deal about a person simply by handling an object which belonged to him. If I were handed a ring or a watch, for example, I could almost feel the object vibrating with the owner's personality. At first, as you might suppose, this seemed rather strange to me, but then I began to wonder why this should not be so.

Surely an object which someone had carried with him would quite naturally be permeated with his feelings and ideas, and these vibrations could even, if carefully interpreted, give a clue to what the person might have ahead of him. I decided to make ESP my vocation. With my newly acquired ambition, I excluded almost all other interests from my mind. I wanted to help people with my gift of psychometry. And now today I am more determined than ever to help others to avoid the pitfalls which I have managed to elude for nearly forty years.

I have always maintained that everyone is gifted in some way. I have spent a great deal of time in meditation and observation, and as a result of this I can at will turn within to find the answers. Regardless of where I might be at the time—in a large room filled with people, on a crowded bus or a busy street corner—I can still tune in on the things that I wish to know.

No doubt some of you are thinking that such tuning in must be very difficult to accomplish. It isn't really, but until I was thoroughly convinced that I had mastered the process, I often wondered if the day would ever come when I would be able to tell others how to tune in.

To me, the ability to tell a person his or her name via psychometry means absolutely nothing. I feel such parlor tricks are a waste of valuable psychic energy, which only informs the client of something he already knows. To what avail is it to be able to tell someone his name is John or her name is Mary? If he has forgotten his name, he can check his driver's license, not a clairvoyant.

Whenever anyone asks me to describe the contents of his wallet or pocket, I inevitably freeze up. These simple tests mean nothing to me, and on such occasions, I am afraid that I am rather blunt. I inform these amateur parapsychologists that I am certain our time can be used to better advantage for something *really* important.

I have a friend in Chicago who can give names, pass on descriptions, read ballots, and so forth, and who is very accurate. This person is absolutely genuine, but she is a Spiritualist. I am not.

When you first begin to psychometrize an article, such as a hairpin, letter, earring, I would suggest that you speak spontaneously. Do not hesitate to say just exactly what comes to your mind. There is no need to concentrate long, or even to think hard; in fact, the secret lies in just being spontaneous, immediately saying what comes to you. Sometimes, however, this can be a little embarrassing, as something of a very intimate nature could come to you, but if you truly feel the urge to speak frankly, you should do so.

I am exceedingly happy and pleased that generally people have accepted me more or less in the role of a counselor as well as a friend. In the many years that I have acted in this capacity, I have yet to meet anyone who misconstrued my meaning. I am mentioning this now so that you can understand that it is quite possible for very "touchy" things to come forth.

Also, I do not always agree with a client. I feel that to "sooth-say" a person is not proper. For years people have asked my advice, and if I feel they are right, I tell them so; if, on the other hand, I feel they are wrong, I have no compunction whatsoever in disagreeing with them. If they have a desire which I know will never materialize, I do not hesitate to reveal this. Don't you agree with me that it is better to tell a person the truth?

There are many people counseling in this type of work who hesitate to tell clients the truth for fear of losing business. The people who write to me are considered my friends rather than my clients. Should I lose a few of them because of my frank-ness, I still feel I must be honest. The day usually comes, though, when those very same people realize that I was right in what I told them. Then they write me, saying, "I'm sorry I became angry. It was only because everyone else I went to guaranteed me that my wish would be mine." Yet, one's common sense should tell him that *everyone* could not have his wish granted.

I do not have to convince anyone, nor do I try. I feel the proof is in the results of an analysis. Unless a person engages in this type of work very conscientiously, it is far better that he refrain from taking it up. Unless you can be honest, leave it alone.

Others engaged in this kind of work have said many times, "Why not string along with them? You won't see them again."

To me, this is a most repulsive suggestion! I want my friends to feel that they can rely on my advice implicitly and have com-plete confidence in me. Consequently, there are people who have been writing to me consistently for twenty-five years. Many times they did not agree with my analyses. I was not right until time proved I was.

I never urge my clients to write me within a certain period of time. I feel that *they* will know when they wish another analysis. It is important for anyone in this work to actually urge a client to write.

Let us start our first experiment with psychometry. Take an object that belongs to you, something that you have worn or used for some time, such as a compact or a comb that you yourself use exclusively.

Then sit quietly, holding the object. Do not force ideas or concentrate. Have a pad and pencil at your side, and as fast as your thoughts come to you, write them down. There will be times when you will say, "This sounds impossible." Still, write it all down. Do not continue this for too long a period, however.

Many who meet me for the first time have often remarked,"Well, for heaven's sake, you look like an ordinary person!" Of course I do. I have not permitted this work to become an obsession, nor do I wish to be labeled by the phrase, "She foretells the future," or, "Be careful what you think in front of Dorothy."

Don't get me wrong, though. I am extremely proud of my ability as far as psychometry is concerned, and never do I conceal the fact. Were someone to ask me if I did psychometry, I'd say, "Yes, I do," change the subject, and just be myself.

An acquaintance of mine happened to pick up a national magazine for which I write and was greatly amazed when she saw my article. I simply said, "Yes, that's my article," and immediately changed the subject. To me, it is utterly ridiculous for anyone to attempt to look eerie or to give the illusion of being "different."

I think it is most obnoxious for anyone to glorify his own particular talent to others. I am open minded on all subjects. I never venture an opinion on religion. I feel that everyone is entitled to his or her own belief. I have the utmost respect for all religions, and I feel that the all-important thing is that each and every one of us professes *some* religion! But I do not say that your religion is wrong because I have a different one; each is one his own level of consciousness.

Neither do I ever try to prove psychometry. I don't have to. There are too many who can attest to its being accurate. The one Infinite Intelligence is the power responsible for this, not me.

How true are these words from the Bible, "I, of myself, can do nothing." The moment one takes credit or becomes egotistical, the power that guides disappears. To my way of thinking, I am merely an instrument tuned in to receive.

Now that you have set aside the object that you yourself have worn, take another, at the same time jotting down your impressions. Again remember that you are not to concentrate. As fast as the thoughts come, jot them down.

Should you be doing psychometrizing for someone else, you may tell them your impressions, rather than jotting them down.

To illustrate: Someone handed me a very lovely ring. Instantly I felt that the place of the ring's origin was exotic, strange, and mysterious.

The answer was, "Yes, it came from India!"

"Don't tell me now," I said. "I could be swayed in my analysis. Keep in mind what I am telling you, and at the end of the interview, I shall go over it with you."

I had an intense feeling that there was something over which this person was extremely repentant. I advised her to do all she could in an attempt to rectify what I considered entirely improper action on her part.

This person was outwardly giving the impression that she was stubborn, egotistical, and absolutely correct in this action; but I still felt that inwardly she was indeed sorry.

This person did not like my saying she was wrong. She told me why she had done this particular thing, to which I replied that she was still wrong.

All I can do is to advise a person; I cannot make anyone do anything. I very plainly told this person that she had done unjust and malicious things as a result of envy and hate. The result was that this person walked away angry.

A year later, she returned and asked me to accept her apology. I assured her that I was not upset over her attitude. When disagreed with, one does not, or should not, become angry; one states a fact plainly, then forgets it.

If I have the feeling that someone is going to go on a journey, I tell him so. When clients ask how that could possibly be, I merely say that I *feel* travel; how, why, when, I do not know, but they will definitely travel.

Can you see the point I am trying to convey to you? State what you feel, then release it.

On one occasion, someone came to me who intended to commit murder. I felt this, and said so. He freely admitted this intention. Strange as it may seem, I felt no fear of him. I assured him that if he were to go ahead with this crime, he would indeed regret his act, and there most certainly would be no happiness gained whatsoever. Five years later, I again met this person. He told me how extremely happy he was that he had heeded my advice.

So you see the things that can be revealed through psychometry. If someone is deceitful to you, you will definitely feel it. However, you should not become angry, but be grateful for the forewarning. Either you should completely avoid this person, or you should attempt to find out why he is being deceitful.

I never tell people things just to please their vanity or to flatter them. Should someone have a fantastic idea that he will find some buried treasure and should he ask my advice about this (and I feel no treasure exists), I say to him, "Oh, that is simply a fantastic idea! You'd better drop it."

One woman told me that five oil men had urged her to keep digging in a certain location for oil. There would be a great deal of money involved with this project. I told her that there was no oil there, but she completely disregarded my advice, to her later sorrow.

On a few occasions, people have said to me, "Why do you charge for this?"

This may surprise you, but are you aware of the fact that the majority of people have no respect for anything that has no value set upon it? When I was very young, I would accept no fee from anyone. I felt that if I could help people in any way, I was well repaid. What happened? I learned that no one had any respect for my judgement! Some even had the audacity to say, "Well, since you evidently don't value your time, I'll go to Mrs. So-and-So who charges five dollars for ten minutes!"

This remark really made me think. And it is for that reason that I have set a nominal fee, which I feel is within the reach of all. Many times, however, people have generously sent me much more, feeling that I was responsible for their having saved hundreds of dollars through the advice I had given them.

In order to be successful in this work, I feel one should be generous for a good cause. One-tenth of all I receive is given to some charity, hospital, or whatever else I might consider to be worthy. This is a must with me! But neither do I mention the cause to which my tithe goes—that is between myself and our Creator.

For your further experiments with psychometry, use objects belonging to those whom you do not know. Ask friends to loan you their old letters, or ask them to assist you (only be ready to be busy when you do). Remember, respect and value must be placed upon your work. Do not overcharge, however, or act as though you are very important. You are merely an instrument, nothing more. Do not appear as either a master or a mastermind; just be yourself.

Should you suddenly feel a headache which you did not have before, this may be an indication that the person with whom you are working is troubled with headaches. You should then, of course, advise the person to see a physician. I do not believe that one should use these talents for healing unless you are certain that you possess the healing power!

Although you should never attempt to diagnose a condition, it is perfectly all right to say, "You have a headache. Don't let a symptom go on without attention."

If you have the feeling of something falling, advise the person to be careful of an object which could fall on him. When I wrote to one man, I had this feeling, so I warned him to be careful of a chandelier or some heavy object that could become loose and fall. This man later entered a restaurant and was just on the verge of sitting at a table when he noticed there was a large chandelier just overhead. Remembering my warning, he sat at another table instead. Incredible though it may seem, this chandelier actually did fall upon the very table that he had first considered!

If you feel you are riding in an automobile, that means the person will be going to talk a great deal. If you have the feeling that you should be cautious of words, tell the person to be careful of what he says at that time.

If you feel a sheaf of papers in your hand, the thought may flash through your mind, "Should these be signed or not?" Immediately you will know that answer. Perhaps you will now experience an undecided feeling, and whereupon you should advise the person to "think this over before signing." Should you have a feeling of elation, then tell him it is all right to go ahead with these contracts.

Throughout this whole procedure, you cannot guess; this must be something you know. You do not waver; you do not retrace.

Sometimes people say, "Let's start all over again and see if you get the same thing." This I refuse to do, since it is only a waste of my time as well as theirs. Then, too, I have the feeling they are simply trying to test me. My faith is implicit. I do not doubt, and going over and over a session is to no avail!

I can assure you that you will be positively amazed at the results of psychometry. This ability differs greatly from any other facet of the paranormal. You will find skeptics, to be sure, yet even they cannot continue to be skeptical when an impression shows up as being correct.

I urge you to be humble at all times, because if you are not, you are not relying upon the power that directs you but rather on your own power, which is very unreliable. Nor do I call upon those who have passed on. Unless you "see" the actual person in spirit, do not attempt spirit contact as it could be detrimental.

While you are holding an object, you might experience a feeling of dizziness. Again, this means the person for whom you are reading has this same feeling. They should be advised to see a doctor.

If you feel unusually blue and depressed, upsetting news may come to the person.

If you experience the feeling that there are logs ahead of you, blocking your way, this means that an obstacle is keeping something from him which he is desirous of obtaining. Try hard to see this log being removed. If it still remains, it means the obstacle will not be removed for some time. If it appears to dissolve, the condition will clear up almost at once.

Here is something which I consider to be vitally important. Suppose someone comes to you desiring a particular goal. Although he does not tell you what this is, you immediately feel there would be much unhappiness, for, say, four people if he were to have this wish granted. Examine this carefully. Would the results actually be worth hurting four people? Does he really want this, or is it a passing fancy? Be honest, tell the person exactly what you feel.

On many occasions I have said, "Yes, it is possible for you to have this, but do you really feel it is worth hurting so many lives? Would you be very happy over its materializing, knowing it would hurt others?" Usually they change their minds about wanting whatever it was they desired so ardently.

If I feel doubtful of someone attaining the wish he has in mind, I tell him that he will turn away from it of his own accord. People dislike hearing this, of course, and they usually maintain, "Oh no, I won't!"

There are those too who insist upon forcing issues, but I have yet to see anyone who was completely happy after attaining his desire at the expense of hurting others. It just cannot be done. As I have said over and over, the law of retribution really works! I know, of course, that there are those who scoff at this, but the day will come when they too will be convinced of this fact.

In the practice of psychometry, the all-important thing is to be very honest. Although your honesty may not be appreciated at the time your advice is given, I can definitely assure you that it will be at a later date. My files confirm that statement.

Business people can use psychometry to great advantage. Let us say you employ a person. You can hold an article of his (not telling him why) and follow the impression.

Arrogance in a prospective employee is denoted by the object feeling warm in your hand. Greed is denoted by a feeling of nausea. This person will step over others to gain! A calm feeling tells you that the person will do his best and you, in turn, must not take advantage of him.

People have often asked, "Will I live long?" You should never say they will pass on (simply warn about health, warn them to be cautious of accidents, etc.). Never give a date of death: this is not for you to do. Much unhappiness can come from this. You can say you feel a death could result from neglect of taking care of a symptom, but the actual date of death is not to be shown.

You will meet many people who would keep you talking to them for five hours if they possibly could. Here you must be firm. Tell them your impressions, terminate the interview, and that is that. Unless you do this, you are headed for trouble. Remember to keep a balance, as I have remarked throughout this book.

I feel that the day will come when psychometry will be universally relied upon. I hope by that time those who are fraudulent and those who have misled people will have been weeded out, and psychometry will be used only in the correct manner.

Chapter Ten

Destroying the Negative Power of Greed

It will be easy for you to realize and release the negative power of greed when you become fully aware of the positive knowledge within yourself. Greed, like crime, does not pay. You will be forever mindful of that fact once you read this chapter. Once you have conquered greed, you will find that you have brought tranquillity into your ife. You in turn will then be able to help others to avoid greed by providing an example to them.

THERE ARE CERTAIN TYPES of people who, becaue of their greed, will use any method available in order to receive monetary benefit.

Not long ago, in a small California town quite close to the city in which I live, a man pulled into the town square in a camping truck which carried a sign, "New Lincoln—a dollar a chance." Practically everyone in town bought a chance, thinking little of thc dollar which they had gambled. One dollar is not a very large amount of money, but if you multiply it by several thousand, you come up with quite a tidy sum.

The majority of people in this town are rather wealthy businessmen, who commute from larger metropolitan areas, so they felt little risk involved in buying several chances on a new Lincoln. The sponsor of the lottery had a formal drawing and announced the name of the man who held the winning ticket.

"When can I expect my new Lincoln?" asked the excited winner.

"It will be delivered to you in just in a few days," the contest holder told him.

A few days later, the eager winner received a shiny new Lincoln penny in the mail. Enclosed in the envelope was a small typewritten note which proclaimed: "This is your prize."

The cleverly-minded confidence man had not put the world "automobile" on any of his advertisments. The signs simply announced that one might purchase a chance on a new Lincoln. It seems that nothing could be done in regard to this deceit, because the man had delivered what he had promised—a new Lincoln.

The man who practiced this fraud was greedy. He did not want to work for anything in his life. He received money for making fools out of people. You may ask if his plans were not against metaphysical laws. They were, of course, and some day it is a certainty that he will be apprehended, and none of his ill-gotten money will do him any good.

When people are desperate, they may be forced into doing certain things which they would not ordinarily do in order to supply their families with the necessities of life. This is much different from a man who deliberately uses a confidence game in order to further his monetary gains. The law of retribution which he has violated will have to be reckoned with.

Clients write to me and ask why some people who appear to be evil have all the money they wish, while the hard-working, honest person must go without adequate funds. One should not judge too hastily, however. What you do not know is that many wealthy people do a great many good deeds, and in some instances, actually donate a certain amount of their earnings to charitable causes.

It is not for you to be concerned whether or not a certain wealthy man has gained his money in a fraudulent or dishonest manner. If he has been deceitful, he will not keep his wealth for long. The law of retribution will have been set in motion.

Do not be resentful of those who have more material wealth than you do. You have no way of knowing exactly what is in that rich person's heart. A man who has worked hard to gain a million dollars or a man who has inherited his wealth is very often a philanthropist at heart, but he may not make it a practice to publish all his charitable acts in the newspapers. Here again you must use your common sense and not condemn those who have more than you possess. You have the ability, which, if rightfully used, will bring you all the material things that you desire.

Many clients have asked me if it is wrong to pray for money. I do not think that such a supplication is wrong. We live in a world which requires our having material things in order to survive. The Bible promises us that nothing is impossible in our lives if we believe.

I am certain the day will come when people will realize that there are many wonderful things which they can do for one another, whether it is sending a good thought to someone in time of need or merely wishing someone well on his life's way. Such an attitude of good will toward all people would be such a giant step forward in humankind's spiritual evolution.

If you follow the methods which I describe in this book, you will discover that they all may be distilled into this simple dictum: *Look into your own self.* If you do this correctly, you will not in any way be controlled by greed. You will not in any manner wish ill upon your fellow humans, whether they be in a foreign country or living next door to you. *Look into your own self*—and you will find that as you do, you will become more adept in matters of a spiritual nature.

The methods which I have outlined in this book should not in any way conflict with any religious beliefs that you may have, because if you turn first to God for guidance and then use the formulas that I have used within these chapters, you will become a better person than you are today.

I have thousands and thousands of letters on file, unsolicited testimonials. When certain of my clients began to write me, they were cynical, skeptical, and, in many cases, writing things designed to deliberately annoy me. I, of course, did not allow myself to become upset. I merely prayed for guidance for these people and asked that they be made to understand the true purpose and the wonderful avantages of my psychic formulas. In each case, these thousands of people have written again to tell me that my methods have made them better persons, that at last they are able to understand themselves.

We mortals are extremely complex. Therefore, when we understand ourselves we just naturally understand other people a lot better. We can more clearly discern that greed has no place in our lives. When we gain a clear understanding of our purpose in life, we find it impossible to deliberately do anything bad against our fellow men.

Whenever you find yourself materialistic to the degree that your self-interest can hurt another person, pause to look within yourself and give thought to the immutable laws of retribution.

You will, no doubt, tell others how to get what they want out of life through ESP, and I hope you do, because then it will become an endless chain. As you proceed in your studies, you are going to find that the things which formerly appeared so mysterious to you are suddenly as easy to examine as if you were staring at them through a beautifully clean and shining pane of glass.

Chapter Eleven

White Magic Versus Black Magic

Even though this chapter is quite short, your mind will sub-consciously absorb the thoughts that I have placed here, so that you will never find yourself in a state of mind such as that which torments so many thousands of misguided people.

You have no doubt seen many articles on black magic, but how many discussions have you read on white magic?

Recently I have received a great many letters asking me what can be done to avert the negative powers of black magic.

Now there is no denying that a great deal of anguish comes to those who have made themselves more susceptible to black magic by their strong belief in the dark arts. An elementary method of counteracting the effects of negative forces is to enter into the silence of meditation and convince your subconscious mind that it is impenetrable to the arrows of black magic. But by the time most of my clients come to me with tales of sorcery, they are too distraught to discuss psychic self-defense—they want me to protect them at once!

Not long ago, a woman wrote to tell me that she and her family had been cursed by a neighbor woman who practiced black magic. According to my client, she had heard of the woman's powers and had decided that she would attempt to get on her good side. The other neighbors warned my client of the woman and her alleged evil nature, but my client and her family accepted an invitation to enter the woman's home for lunch.

The accused witch served a cake, which everyone pronounced very good. They thanked their hostess and went home. The next day, the husband lost his job, my client suffered severe stomach pains, and their two sons had something terribly unpleasant occur to them that afternoon. All of these things added up to give them the impression that the witch had put something evil into a cake which had been especially designed to bring misery into their lives. They became horribly frightened.

How sad it is that this woman waited twenty years to write to me! Her letter told of how her husband seemed unable to keep a job, her stomach pains continued to torment her, how their sons had become troublesome in school, and how, once out of school, they became poor unemployment risks.

I immediately put her letter ahead of the others in my day's mail and sent her a reply by airmail, special delivery. I advised her that as long as she and her family entertained the idea that they had been hexed, they would suffer another twenty years of misery. If they were to place their faith in God, I told her, and apply the principle of faith to their situation, they would come to realize that no one is given the power to cause so much misery to another person. I admonished her that God, who loves us and is kind, would not allow any group of people to wield negative psychic power which could cause the torment that she described in her letter.

She promised me any amount of money if I would only free them from the witch's curse. I said that I was not interested in financial gain. My only concern was that she and her family remove the negative idea of a hex from their minds and begin to once again lead a normal life. The first thing to do, I instructed her, was to erase all these thoughts of black magic from their minds. I told her to expect only the best, to plan a new beginning for the entire family. Secondly, I asked her to look upon the alleged witch as a fellow human being and to realize that she could be a very good person in the religion which she might follow.

About three months later, the woman wrote to me and said: "It worked, Dorothy! It really worked! What do I owe you?"

I replied that I had only one fee for an analysis, and since she had already sent this, there would be no further charge. I was only happy that things had worked out so well for her and her family.

Later, I heard again from the woman, and she informed me that she and the "witch" had become good friends. My client had gone to the neighbor and told of the misery which had plagued her and her family for twenty years.

The "witch's" eyes had filled with tears, and she said, "If you had only known that I liked you as a friend, and in fact the night that you came over and had that cake with me, I had every good thought in mind that we could have a wonderful relationship. I often wondered why you never again came into my home."

Chapter Twelve

ESP Can Work for You

As I have stated before, everyone has a certain degree of ESP.
In this chapter I will demonstrate how ESP can be developed.

J F YOU SINCERELY WISH to develop your ESP, you must not attempt to induce it by abnormal physical and psychical conditions. Under no circumstances should you seek to artificially stimulate ESP abilities by ingesting drugs or inhaling chemical vapors. If any dubious teacher of psychic development should suggest that you accompany him on a "trip" with LSD or one of the hallucinogenic drugs, I hope that you will turn and walk away from him. All true psychics are vigorous in their denunciation of drugs. We humans have all that we need within ourselves. Chemical stimulants only lead to false teachings and harmful practices.

To take drugs is to take a downward step in your psychic growth. You do not need artificial means to bring forth the ESP which already lies dormant within your psyche.

As I have mentioned previously, I am not too keen about even the trance state as a means of summoning one's ESP abilities. I personally have never allowed myself to go into a trance when I am preparing someone's analysis.

People carry a certain atmosphere of their own characteristics composed primarily of mental and emotional vibrations. Subconsciously, everyone feels subtle differences when he confronts various types of people. Certainly such differences in atmosphere are very apparent when one enters a strange house or a church or a supermarket—each location emits an atmosphere which is distinctly its own.

Ministers, attorneys, public speakers in general are quite aware of the fact that each audience holds it own atmosphere. When the actor walks on stage, the preacher steps to the pulpit, the attorney moves forward to state his case, they immediately feel the almost palpable atmosphere that surrounds each and every crowd.

Have you ever walked down the street of a little town and felt calm and contented? Upon investigation, you would almost certainly find that this small town is known for the friendliness of its good people.

If you step into a room where people are attuned to your thoughts, you feel no conflict. If you are to be the speaker before such an audience, you instantly feel very calm. You are at once more sure of yourself because the people in the audience are projecting their warmth to you.

So many new students of metaphysics ask me why we are not overwhelmed with the force of so many people constantly transmitting psychic vibrations. Why do we not become so confused with all the several separate messages and simply lose all the effect of these transmissions?

While it is true that we are more or less affected by the multitude of psychic vibrations beating upon us, the greater part of these messages do not consciously impress us.

Let me give you an example: When you walk down a busy street, you do not consciously hear every automobile that passes you. You do not hear every truck and distinguish its louder engine from that of a sports car. If you should enter a crowded store, you would not hear every word that was said around you from the mouths of dozens of people.

We only hear and see the things that attract our attention and interest. All the rest is lost to us.

When we mix black and white, we produce the neutral color of gray. Several currents of opposing thought vibrations tend to resolve themselves into neutral vibrations that will have little or no effect upon those sensitive individuals coming into contact with them.

The character of your thoughts and feelings actually repels vibrations which are inharmonious to your basic nature. All those who have studied metaphysical laws are aware that one draws thought vibrations which are in harmony with his own and repels those vibrations which are of a contrary nature.

If you should find yourself in a room with a person about whom you really know very little, but you suddenly feel as if you would like to run far, far away, you may be assured that his thoughts do not gravitate on the same plane as yours and that you would be wrong to cultivate a friendship with this person.

At this point, I would like to quote from the address which Sir William Crookes gave before the Royal Society of England in 1898. Sir William, a prominent chemist and definer of physical laws, reported on ESP in a bold manner to an assemblage of distinguished scientists:

> Were I now introducing for the very first time these inquiries to the world of science, I should choose a starting point different from that of the old (where we formerly began). It would be well to begin with telepathy; with that fundamental law as I believe it to be, that thoughts and images may be transferred from one mind to another without the agency of the recognized organs of sense, that knowledge may enter a human mind without being communicated in any hitherto known or recognized way. If telepathy takes place, we have two physical facts: a physical change in the brain A, the suggestor, and the analogous physical change in the brain of B, the recipient of the suggestion. Between these two physical events there must exist a train of physical causes. It is unscientific to call in the aid of mysterious agencies, when with every fresh advance in knowledge it is shown that ether vibrations have powers and attributes abundantly able to any demand—even the transmission of thought.

It is supposed by some physiologists that the essential cells of nerves do not actually touch, but they seem to be separated by a narrow gap which widens in sleep while it narrows almost to extension during mental activity. This condition is so singularly like a Branly or Lodge coherer [a device which led to the discovery of the wireless telegraphy] as to suggest a further analogy. The structure of brain and nerve cells being similar, it is conceivable that there may be present such masses of nerve coherers in the brain, whose special function it may be to receive impulses brought from without through the connecting sequence of either waves of appropriate order of magnitude.

Roentgen has familiarized us with an order of vibrations of extreme minuteness as compared with the smallest waves which we will have hitherto been acquainted and there is no reason to suppose that we have here reached the limit of frequency. It is known that the action of thought is accompanied by certain molecular movements of the brain and here we have physical vibrations capable from their extreme minuteness of acting direct upon the individual's molecules. While the rapidity approaches that of internal, an external movement of the items themselves, a formidable range of phenomena must be scientifically stifled before we effectively grasp a fact so strange, so bewildering and for ages so inscrutable as to the direct action of mind upon mind.

In the old Egyptian days a well-known inscription was carved over the portal of the Temple of Isis; "I am whatever has been, is or ever will be; and my veil hath no man yet lifted."

Not thus do modern seekers after truth confront nature, the word that stands for the baffling mysteries of the universe…Steadily and unstintingly we strive to pierce the inmost heart of nature…to reconstruct what she has been and to prophesy what she will be. Veil after veil have we lifted and her face grows more beautiful, august and wonderful with every barrier that is withdrawn.

Sir William Crookes investigated the higher forms of psychic phenomena with results that startled the world. But you will notice that he does not attempt to give any other than purely physical laws the credit for the phenomenon of telepathy. He also escaped the common error of confusing physical phenomena with the phenomena of the astral senses. Remember, each plane of consciousness has its own phenomena. That is why when you meet people, you encounter them on the level of consciousness that you have each acquired.

Thought vibrations set up a rather peculiar reaction in the substance of the pineal gland, and this could be the very first step in the transformation of the vibrations to thought forms. It is always interesting to see what results you may attain from sending forth and receiving mental and emotional waves of force.

There are some experimenters who form a cup with the fingers of their left hand, as if they have been holding a ball and have then removed it. The imaginary ball leaves the left hand, and then the right arm is held out while the experimenter thinks strongly of the person whom they wish to contact. When they feel a certain tingle in their right arm, they are convinced that they have contacted their target. I myself have tried this little experiment many times, and it certainly seems to work.

To achieve success in any ESP experiment, it is important to keep your mind on a high level of consciousness. In this manner, you will know that which you send out to people is good. ESP is not allotted only to a chosen few; if you take the time to follow the exercises as I have outlined them within the pages of this book, ESP can work for you.

I do not believe that it is necessary to practice deep breathing or to "go out of this world" in a trance to experience any facet of ESP. You should follow my suggestions, then just relax and let things happen. You will probably find that your life will change once you have revitalized these dormant ESP faculties and allowed them to take over.

When you have a hunch, you will soon learn to recognize when you should follow it and when you should not. If the hunch is a negative one, you will experience a little hesitancy. You will have a feeling of being held back, and that always means that there are certain elements of alarm connected with the hunch. You will learn to know when to move slowly and when you should act upon your intuition with all haste.

You will find that as you learn to use ESP you will be able to enter a streetcar or a bus and tell instantly which of your fellow passengers are on the same level of consciousness that you are. This is a wonderful feeling, because you know at once that you can trust these people. You know that you are all tuned in on the same wavelength.

There are many people today who do not feel that they should develop their ESP or that they should even read books on the subject. They are blocked by superstition and fear, and in some cases they feel that the development of one's extrasensory abilities is against the teachings of the Bible. To such charges, I always answer that ESP, if used correctly, puts God first in one's life.

If you set about developing your psychic abilities, you need not fear that you are going to hear voices or anything like that. After you read this book, I hope that the words will have become so implanted in your subconscious that every time you have a hunch you will pause for a moment and wait for that certain feeling which will tell you whether or not to proceed. You will be able to keep everything under perfect control at all times.

There is no harm in using crystal balls, cards, or any other physical object as a guide post. Bear in mind, however, that the crystal or whatever you wish to use is only a means of placing your mind in a state which will allow you to proceed with that which you wish to know. The power, in other words, lies within you, not within the cards or the crystal ball.

I am certain that as time goes on there will be many wonderful steps forward in the scientific study of ESP. By the year 2100 I suspect that we today will seem rather primitive as far as our study of the mind is concerned.

I also feel that as more and more attention is being directed toward the field of metaphysics, there will be those individuals who will seek to misuse the certain meager talents which have been granted to them. They will, however, only be permitted to abuse their abilities to a limited degree. They will suddenly find that no more power will come to them. Their minds will become blank. Divine Intelligence, with its immutable law, will soon make it impossible for those unscrupulous ones to go on abusing their gifts.

The higher intelligence is as impersonal as an electrical outlet. If you plug in a light bulb into it, you get light. If you stick your finger into it, you get a shock. You could stick your finger in there a dozen times a day and a dozen times a day you would receive a shock, because you would not be using the outlet for the purpose for which it was intended. If the most brilliant and accomplished electrician were to stick his finger into the outlet, he too would receive a shock. Like the electrical outlet, Divine Intelligence is no respecter of persons. Those who seek to use it for improper purposes will be "shocked" into withdrawal by immutable laws.

If you misuse your body, you will pay for your abuses by suffering ill health. If you misuse your gift of ESP, you will pay for your lack of stewardship by setting in motion the laws of psychic retribution.

One does not really get away with a thing in life. Some may think they do, but some day there will be the piper to pay. Remember that retribution awaits these violators of the universal laws. We must not be guilty of passing judgment upon them ourselves.

Many times I have known through ESP that certain people were guilty of certain acts which were very wrong. My human self condemned these people, and I have made angry remarks that an indignant human being would make. But from a strictly practical point of view, I found that I am not able to carry on with my work if I hold condemnation against anyone. From both the ideal and the practical viewpoints, I learned that it is not for me to judge others.

I may feel upset; I may wish I could warn the person about what he is doing to himself; but the violator himself has the power within his own psyche to stop using his gifts in a negative manner.

My daughter has confessed that many times when she was much younger she would ignore the warnings which I could foresee for her. Many of my clients have assumed that because I am in this work, nothing adverse will ever happen to my family. They feel that I should be able to guide my family around every pitfall because of my superior insight and knowledge. This is not completely true, because my family and I are merely human beings. Even though I warned my daughter completely and accurately, she often did not listen, but went right on ahead with her plans. Regardless of how I had cautioned her against certain choices in her life, she had to go through these sad experiences until she learned her lesson.

I could warn my daughter, but I could not live her life for her. Only the other day she said that if only young people might realize that the law of retribution passes no one by, they might be able to mature with much less pain. But she, in spite of my forewarnings, chose to make her own decisions and suffer the consequences. Perhaps these particular experiences were necessary for her spiritual growth.

The day will come, I am certain, when even those people who today consider ESP as fortune-telling quackery or the work of the devil will see the value in developing one's extrasensory talents. I feel that there have been times in the past when some people have misconstrued my work, but they did not hesitate to follow my advice. I know what I am doing. I know within my heart whether I am right with people or not, and I am completely frank when people write for an analysis.

If I were some sideshow fortune-teller, I would tell each of my clients that everything was coming their way, but I don't think anyone who has ever contacted me can accuse me of such superficial guidance. People often become stubborn when I recommend a certain course of action, but they usually write back at a later date and tell me that my advice was correct. When I tell you this, I do so in all humility, because it is not I who guides my clients, but the Divine Intelligence with which I am in tune.

ESP has made me more sensitive to other people's wants and needs. They do not have to tell me their desires. In some manner, their unspoken words always manage to reach my inner ears. It is always rather surprising to my clients when they have yet to say a word and I tell them about the matters which concern them.

If you should develop a high degree of ESP, you must vow to always guide people truthfully and to retain your humility. Never try to convince people that you are a special kind of mortal. Advise people to wake up their own slumbering ESP abilities, and in time you will hear folks saying to each other, "Pardon me, your ESP is showing!"

Chapter Thirteen

Negative Thoughts Anonymous

This title may seem a bit unusual, but stop and think for a moment. You have no doubt heard of Alcoholics Anonymous, Gamblers Anonymous, Smokers Anonymous, and as I concentrate on these words, I think a very worthwhile idea has been born. Why not a Negative Thoughts Anonymous?

IF YOU HAVE STUDIED METAPHYSICS at all in depth, you know that your thoughts are living things. Positive thoughts strengthen the individual, while negative thoughts can gnaw away at people until they are destroyed by them. What should you do when you are being horribly beleaguered by negative thoughts?

Members of Alcoholics Anonymous are able to call one another when they feel themselves weakening to the thirst for alcohol. They are thus able to fortify one another by talking the weakness out of their systems. Think how wonderful it would be to be able to call someone when you find yourself beset by negative thoughts. If you are able to telephone someone who was in harmony with right thinking, he or she might be able to set your mind at ease with just the right words. Can you think of some people in your area whom you might call when negative thoughts assail you? And you, too, must be ready to come to their aid when they are battling dark thoughts. How wonderful if you were able to set up such a bond with a positive-thinking friend just as soon as you finished reading this chapter.

Think of the times when you have awakened in the morning feeling rather blue and discouraged. That would be the time to reach for the telephone and dial your "thought pal." After you have done this, it is almost inconceivable that, after hanging up, you would not feel better.

This is not Pollyannaish thinking; this is something I have tried with great success with a great many people. Most of the time I did not even tell my friends what I was doing. I merely called them when I felt blue and talked to them. I did not say that negative thoughts had been battering at me and ask them to give me a lift. But nine times out of ten, my friends said something inspiring, perhaps unconsciously on their part, without realizing the boost they were giving me.

If you should begin to make a practice of calling someone when you are blue and then tell one other person about this technique, I would guess that within a short time you would have quite a circle of people gathered together in your own Negative Thoughts Anonymous. I would not suggest that you have meetings or dues—unless you feel this would be desirable for some specific purpose—but an occasional informal meeting might serve as an added bit of inspiration for your group.

As a rule, I do not believe that you should ever go into a long, drawn-out conversation as to what your problem is. I definitely feel that it would be better to simply call a "thought pal," say that you are somewhat depressed, and just talk until you feel better.

If you have a friend who would react to Negative Thoughts Anonymous by asking, "Why should I be bothered by someone calling me and telling me her problems?" it is apparent that she does not belong in your circle. This person simply would not be on the same trend of consciousness as the rest of you.

You will be able to tell by the tone of a person's voice that moment you call them whether or not they would be able to provide you with the needed bit of elation and inspiration. If the tone is the least bit icy, make a polite excuse and do not call them again when you are depressed.

Be certain that the people you call understand the law of thought. If your friend is on the same level of consciousness as you are, I can guarantee you that you might begin talking about something as innocuous as the weather, not even telling him that you are depressed, and he will say something that will precisely fit your particular problem.

If a person is truly in tune, he will know by the very fact that you are calling him that you are throwing out a lifeline, wanting someone en rapport with you to grab hold of the other end. He will know that you want someone to help change your negative thoughts into positive ones.

I have used this method many times and I know that it works. I wanted so very much to put this technique into this book because I know that you will experience a wonderful kind of oneness if you begin to practice Negative Thoughts Anonymous with your friends. Once this mental togetherness has been achieved, you will be able to call members of your circle at any time and they will only have to say "Be of good cheer" to immediately redirect your mind to the positive side.

Again I suggest that you do not encourage people who call you to go into much detail about their problems. The more you learn of a problem, the more you may be inclined to make judgments or to criticize the course of action which your "thought pals" have taken. They have called for sympathy, elevation, and inspiration, not for a lecture.

I feel that my brain child of Negative Thoughts Anonymous could be extremely profitable to those who would use it correctly. After a time, I can assure you, you will pick up the telephone less and less, as you revert back to your own solid positive thinking. As each day goes by, you will be growing in more complete awareness and in more total consciousness.

Dale Hamilton wrote in *Country Living and Country Thinking* that "Every person is responsible for only the good within his abilities and for no more, and no one can tell whose sphere is the largest."

I can foresee Negative Thoughts Anonymous growing larger and larger in the years ahead. I can foresee that when "thought pals" get together they will not have to discuss personal problems. They will have a perfect understanding, a union between them, that will mature into a beautiful relationship.

I hope that no one will appropriate this idea of mine with the thought of making money from it. Negative Thoughts Anonymous should be used only voluntarily among friends who are on the same level of consciousness. But I know that the people who read this book will be, almost without exception, the honest and the upright. If they were not people of high caliber, they would not have been of a sufficient level of consciousness to purchase a book with this title in the first place!

Thomas Hood say, "A moment's thinking is an hour in words." How true. Therefore, the more I think about it, the more I am convinced that Negative Thoughts Anonymous was born out of the urgency of my many clients who have asked me to write this book. Somehow I knew that there would be something "extra" added to the text that I did not have in mind when I started this project. If this book should launch the movement of Negative Thoughts Anonymous into active being, then I will be happy, because I know that it will bring so much comfort and happiness to those who use it properly.

Chapter Fourteen

Your Pushbutton Control

This chapter describes a method which will allow you to be the master of every situation in but a few moments' time. There is no magical computer offered here, but a technique that is as modern and streamlined as our latest electronic control devices—and just as accurate.

AS YOU READ THIS CHAPTER, I want you to visualize little red buttons set in a row, and I will show you how to use them in a most revolutionary way. This volume is not really a textbook, but it is a book that can automatically bring about both mental and material changes in your life. That is one reason why I ask you to keep this book by your bedside, and after you have carefully read it through, make a habit of re-examining a few pages each night. You will find that you absorb a great deal in those last few moments before you drift off to sleep.

Since this is a materialistic world, the majority of you will want me first to describe how to use your pushbutton control for money.

Reread the chapter on visualization. Next, picture a panel of red buttons set in a row—oh, let us say on a piece of mahogany about nine inches long and about four inches wide. Make it a very beautiful piece of mahogany, rich and glistening with expensive polish.

Now visualize that one of these buttons is marked "Money." If I were to tell you that you had access to all the money you could ever desire, or if I told you that you could buy anything you wanted by pushing this button, what would you say? You would protest that you did not believe me, that such a notion was impossible. But in your mind's eye you can have anything you want.

Each night at bedtime, reread or skim the visualization chapter, underline passages in the book, make notes in the margins. Then lie back on you pillow, click off your bedlamp, close your eyes, and in your mind's eye, push down the button marked "Money." This should cause a noticeable reaction in your body, because if you truly believe as I am telling you to do, you will feel very relaxed. And you will feel very wealthy. You will feel as if all your financial wants have been satisfied.

It is not wrong to desire money if you do not intend to misuse it in any manner. So many people misquote the Bible and say that money is the root of all evil. These self-appointed evangelists leave out one extremely important word: as I pointed out earlier, the Bible warns us that the *love* of money is the root of all evil.

I think you can easily see the difference in meaning. You do not love money; you do not worship it or adore it; you do not desire it for immoral purposes; you do not wish to hoard it. You wish to have money to obtain the material things you want out of life, and you want to be generous with your money to those people, who for one reason or another, are less fortunate than you.

Perhaps the button that would rank next in popularity for the most number of people is the one marked "Love."

Remember first of all that you have to give love in order to receive it. You must be prepared to give physical love and spiritual devotion to the person whom you wish to marry in order to receive the complete fulfillment of love.

As you see your prospective mate in his true light and realize that he is the one whom you love, you will lose a certain amount of tension. You will find yourself going out of your way to please him. He in turn cannot help feeling the same way toward you, because subconsciously he will be attuned to your emanations of love.

Many wives write me and say that they are infuriated with their husbands. I advise them to sit down calmly and not to condemn the man to whom they are married, but to draw up a list of his good points. He must have some good points or they would not have married him.

"Oh, but he has changed!" some women wail. "He just isn't the same person."

If you are one of those women who have drawn up a list of complaints against your husband, stop and consider for a moment if he might not feel that you too have changed.

Pause to look at your husband in the light in which you saw him before you were married. Recapture some of that interior glow of the courting period. Allow these romantic thoughts to permeate your entire attitude. Your husband will not be able to ignore the change which will have come over you.

Soon you will find that all tension will have been released where the person you love is concerned. You will feel more certain of yourself. You will be as you once were—a dynamic personality who gives as well as takes. And, while you have been working this inner magic upon yourself, you will be pleased to observe that you will also have accomplished a transformation upon your husband.

Sex plays a very important role in any good marriage, but so many unfortunate people come to the point where they feel they have lost interest in their mate as a love partner. Often this is not because they have found another romantic interest, but because they feel their mate has lost interest in them. Here, too, if you are a woman, do not neglect those certain little ways that a woman has of letting her man know how much he means to her.

For any reader who wishes the love of a prospective partner who is "right," or who wishes to regain the love that once warmed their marriage, picture in detail the situation which you desire and visualize yourself interacting with your loved one. Again, before you fall asleep at night, push the red button labeled "Love."

Some of you may feel you lack a sufficient number of friends to suit your psychic and emotional needs. Visualize new people coming into your life, press down the red button marked "Friends," and you will be amazed at the number of mysterious ways in which new friends will begin to enter your own little world. And you may be assured that these new people will be the right kind of people for you, because you and your push-button control will have been on the proper level of consciousness to attract similar personalities.

Once you begin to use your pushbutton control, you will discover an enormous number of potentialities within you that you have not begun to take advantage of.

I can hear some readers complaining that they are very busy people. How, they ask, can we ever master time?

Whether you are rushing on the corner of State and Madison in Chicago, or scurrying on Broadway and Seventh in Los Angeles, here is a special pushbutton marked "Time." If you need extra minutes, take the time to visualize your control board and the red "Time" button. In your mind's eye, calmly push it down.

If you have visualized properly, your subconscious should now come into play and begin to point out where you can save a minute or two by eliminating certain waste motion on your part. It will point out useless, time-consuming habits. It will caution you against making certain futile, time-swallowing stops on your agenda.

You will be able to go on to your next appointment looking as if you did not have a care in the world. You will have mastered time, and the client who greets you will warm to the feeling of self-confidence that generates from you. You will arrive appearing well-groomed, unhurried, and self-assured, instead of puffing into the office disheveled and tense.

And, amazingly, you will find at the end of the work day that you have as much as an hour "left over" from your schedule— sixty minutes which you may use in any manner you so desire.

Suppose you become depressed. Regardless of how great a positive thinker you may be or how much you may be utilizing your psychomagnetism, I will say that there will be times when you will be depressed.

Now a "Despair" button wouldn't look too happy, would it? Put a black surface on that button. But then, when you push down on the "Despair" button, immediately "erase" that black surface and replace it with a bright red sheen like the others.

Here is another trick to use in combatting depression: Utilize that feeling of lethargy that comes with despair by relaxing yourself from the tip of your toes to the top of your head. Make use of that loggy feeling to allow your body to rest and mend itself. Permit your nerves to untwist. Begin to build up a new reserve of energy. Know that you will be the master and will gain full control of the situation.

By erasing the black surface from the "Despair" button, you will have turned depression into a growing sense of confidence. Despair will leave you because you will have become so busy with new projects—after you have taken advantage of the temporary lethargy by permitting yourself to relax completely.

Once you make a regular practice of converting despair into opportunity, you will soon find that depression will become less and less evident in your life.

Another rather dark button on your pushbutton control is marked "Rough Blows."

We will know that we are going to be faced by a certain amount of sickness. We may already have been made acutely aware of the fact that our loved ones will, in time, pass on, as will we.

When a loved one has completed his mission here on earth, use your pushbutton control to help make you accept the fact that your loved one has merely entered a room with a closed door that prevents you from asking the direct contact that had been so important to you.

You will be able to rise above such crises and use your pushbutton control to open new avenues in your life.

Suppose you wish to achieve an important goal. Visualize that goal in detail in your mind's eye, then push down the red button marked "Success." Practice visualization, relax, and picture yourself attaining that goal. The moment you lie back and press that "Success" button, know that you have set in action the thing which you most want to occur.

If you have lacked stamina and vigor, you may mark one of your red buttons with the label "Energy." Remember to relax first, then concentrate on revitalizing those tired nerves, muscles, and sluggish limbs. You are fully capable of commanding the things which you want.

Another little red button which is extremely important to some people is the one marked "Sleep." If you suffer from insomnia and dread going to bed for another miserable night of tossing and turning, follow these instructions carefully.

First, relax your toes until they feel very light, so light that you are certain that they are floating away. You cannot allow your toes to float away without the rest of your foot, so now picture your foot attaching itself to your airborne toes.

Continue this "floating" procedure with the remainder of your body—your legs, your thighs, your knees, right on up until you get to the top of your head. By this time you should feel very relaxed.

Do not keep telling yourself to go to sleep. Your total relaxation should have dispelled all restless thoughts, so that by the time you have reached your neck and shoulders, sleep should not be far away.

Remember always to take full advantage of your pushbutton control. It will work in every department of your life. Soon you will be able to add your own little pushbuttons to that attractive piece of mahogany that you have formed in your mind's eye, and before you know it, you will have become extremely adept at pushing fears and tensions out of your life. You will become so relaxed, so contented, that you will appear years younger.

As you continue deeper in your study of psychomagnetism and the paranormal, you will come to help others along the path of life. I do hope you will recommend that they read this book so that it may also become their personal guide and companion and serve them as well as I pray it has served you.

To order additional copies of this book,
please send full amount plus $4.00 for
postage and handling for the first book and
50¢ for each additional book.

Send orders to:

Galde Press, Inc.
PO Box 460
Lakeville, Minnesota 55044-0460

Credit card orders call 1–800–777–3454
Phone (952) 891–5991 • Fax (952) 891–6091
Visit our website at www.galdepress.com

Write for our free catalog.